Dieter Graf

Walking
on
Samos

GW00722368

Hiking and Swimming for Island-Connoisseurs
25 Walks with GPS data

Graf Editions

Using this illustrated walking guide

AWT stands for Actual Walking Time. This time does not include breaks, wrong turns or sight-seeing. The AWT serves as a personal control as to whether certain route markings, emphasized in **bold print**, have been reached in the given time. These times are an aid for orientation and should not be considered as encouragement to achieve a record performance. Spot heights are added in brackets.

The approximate **overall length** of a walk is specified in hours in the introduction to each tour. These figures do not include time taken for bus trips or extra-long breaks. Information concerning the **length of the walks**, the **difference in altitude** and three **levels of difficulty** can also be found there.

Route photos are intended for orientation, for consulting locals and as a stimulus. The corresponding text is marked by ① to ④. The **route sketches** have been drawn to the best of our knowledge but lay no claim to completeness.

GPS points are shown as P in texts and on maps. Map datum WGS84.

We would be grateful for useful information concerning **changes** in paths and similar data. As a token of our appreciation we will send you a free copy of our next edition.

The website www.graf-editions.de informs you of any changes that occur along walking routes.

The author **Dieter Graf** is an architect who has travelled all over the world. He has walked the Aegean Islands since the years when tourism was just beginning there and is considered a connoisseur of the islands.

© 2013 Edition Dieter Graf, Elisabethstr. 29, 80796 Munich, Germany
Tel. 0049-(0)89-271 59 57, Fax 0049-(0)89-271 59 97
www.graf-editions.de

All rights reserved.

Type-Setting: Michael Henn, Reichenschwand · Maps: Kurt Zucher, Markt Indersdorf
Translation: Myles Oliver, Muenchen

Original Title: Wandern auf Samos (ISBN 978-3-9814047-2-2)
Dutch Title: Wandelen op Samos (ISBN 978-3-9814047-4-6)

Cover photo: Ayios Konstantínos ⑱

ISBN 978-3-9814047-3-9

Contents

	Walks					Page

Sámos

One of the ancient names of Sámos was Stephane, the "Island of abundance"; it was also called "Flowery", "Virginal", "Cypress-rich" – all of which still applies today. The abundance of water and the gentle moulding of the landscape have given rise to one of the most fertile islands in the Aegean. Sámos' variety of landscapes is unique: united here are forests with pines, oaks and planes, terraced vineyards, concealed springs and what is more, at 1,143 m, the highest mountain in the Aegean, the Kérkis.

Sámos lies in the Ionian settlement area of Antiquity, the cradle of Greek culture. In the sixth pre-Christian millennium Sámos' ruler Polycrates led the island to the first cultural, political and economic blossoming of ancient Greece which 100 years later reached its peak in Athens.

After many millennia of decline and foreign domination the island is slowly beginning to develop. Tourism also plays a major role here, apart from agriculture. However it has shaped Sámos a lot less than other Greek islands. There are hardly any major hotel complexes. The visitor still finds an island characterised by the Greek-Mediterranean way of life.

Especially for hikers Sámos is an eldorado. One wanders through fertile valleys, shady oak forests and age-old olive groves and climbs steep cliffs and karstic mountain tops – with distant views of the surrounding islands. For bathing one comes across extensive sandy beaches and hidden rocky coves. And in the villages one can still encounter the unspoilt Greece with its friendly people and their hospitality, or "filoxenía".

Particularly worthwhile is the north coast with wooded slopes and vineyards which continue to be criss-crossed by old mule tracks. But the destinations described in this book also include old monasteries and the archaeological sites around Pythagório. Unforgettable is the endless light in Greece, the blue sea, the beaches, the paved paths and the spicy scent of thyme, sage and oregano. Not to mention the simplicity and stillness which are part and parcel of the hiking experience.

Have a good trip!   *Kaló taxídi!*

Walking on Sámos

Sámos is, thanks to its position in front of the mountains of Asia Minor, blessed with sufficient precipitation. The vegetation is correspondingly luscious, making the islands an ideal hiking region. Moreover, the hiker still finds many intact **old mule tracks.** For centuries these narrow *monopátia* used to help the farmers work the fields and, up until 30 years ago, formed a dense network of tracks.

By contrast, the up to four metre wide paved tracks, the *kalderímia,* connected larger villages for the transport of goods and served as paths for pilgrims to the monasteries (p. 41). They were paved with marble. Some of them are said to be up to 1000 years old.

Motorisation has not failed to leave its mark on the islands either. Instead of mules the farmers now use pickups, which require wider roadways. The old network of tracks was torn apart by broadening the mule tracks to make them accessible to cars wherever it seemed to be necessary and by pushing aside the characteristic dry walls along the waysides, all co-financed by money from the European Union Regional Funds. The remaining paths are now superfluous and in ruins and are gradually being forgotten by the islanders. Lately, however, the EU Leader Fund provides money to restore some of the remaining mule tracks, mainly for the sake of tourism. Instead of maintaining and extending the scope of the network, however, this often only amounts to the over-perfect restoration of individual paths. This book aims to help ensure that the old mule tracks which still exist are used again and hence preserved before they are irreparably destroyed. They may, above all in spring, be rather overgrown!

The routes described have been walked along again shortly before publication and can be followed without difficulty by people in normal physical condition. Some of the walks are suitable for children. Special surefootedness is not necessary. The √ markings in the text concern only those who are very afraid of heights. For longer walking tours **short cuts** are indicated. Due to the good views, the tours normally lead from the mountains to the sea – so take along your swimming gear. You should be absolutely sure to pick a nice day for tours in the mountains since there is always the danger of sudden fog formation. Moreover it can rain there even in summer. On the other hand there is a risk of forest fires in the summer. In the large fire of 2000 one third of the forest was burned. The scars have still not entirely healed. If you want to walk alone, you should by all means leave information in your hotel and save the number of the hotel on your mobile phone. In order to get your blood circulation going, you should begin leisurely for the first fifteen minutes and, during the tour, eat and especially drink often, even if you don't feel the need to do so. The route maps show springs and wells to be found by the wayside. Be sure to protect yourself sufficiently against sun and wind too.

Coloured dots and arrows can often be found as **markings along paths**, but they do not necessarily correspond to the descriptions in this book. In addition there are the wooden signs and little red-and-white metal signs of the Greek organisations. Old tracks are partly marked above all on the north coast. There are road maps available and, recently, **walking maps** too, for example from the Greek publishing houses Road, Rama and Skaï. As new roadways continue to be built, it may be that the route descriptions are partly out of date, thus calling for certain **orientation skills.** If you have orientation problems, you should always ask the locals about the "monopáti", otherwise you will be directed to roads for vehicular traffic. Mule dung on the narrow paths is more certain to lead you further than goat droppings since the goat paths usually end somewhere in the scrub, while mules always return to their stalls. If you lose your way, you may have to shin up a field wall or climb over steel mesh used as grazing fences with the help of a pile of stones. Some pasture fences are knotted shut on the side where there are two perpendicular rods. You owe it to the farmers whose land you walk across to shut the openings again afterwards, of course. Access to the sea is allowed in Greece as a matter of principle.

The north coast has a well developed bus network, thus making it easy to reach all the destinations from one base. The walks on the south side can be reached from beach accommodations in Pythagório and Votsalákia or with a hire car.

Almost all the starting and finishing points are served by public buses, even in the low season. In case a service does not operate, take a taxi. The drivers are obliged to switch on the taximeter. A possibility for circular walking tours is a relatively reasonable rental car or a rental motor bike. In addition, car drivers also enjoy taking along a wanderer who waves him down.

Despite some efforts having been taken, environmental protection still remains an unsolved problem, so a few of the things you see lying around while walking through the countryside will not always correspond to your sense of order and environmental stipulations.

Sufficient **hiking gear** includes a backpack for a day, shoes with good soles (no sandals), comfortable socks, long trousers or zipper trousers*, a mobile phone possibly, binoculars, a whistle, a small flashlight and picnic equipment with a salt-shaker. In the spring and fall, rain gear is a necessity. A GPS device or a compass would also be good but is not necessary if you have a somewhat good sense of orientation.

*The legs of zipper trousers which also have vertical zippers can be zipped together to form a pad to sit on at the beach. And if you connect both zippers, you have a chic skirt for visiting monasteries.

Climate and Walking Season

The typical, temperate Mediterranean climate with a hot summer and mild, rainy winter predominates on Sámos. The maximum **air temperature** is 32 °C in August (at night 22 °C). In the winter the temperature sinks to 13 °C (6 °C) in February. Snow can fall once or twice a year in the mountains over 1000 m high and lie there for a short while.

The **water temperatures** are lowest in February at 16 °C and reach an almost subtropical 25 °C in August. You can go swimming from the end of May at 19 °C through October (22 °C).

The mountains in Asia Minor help Sámos to get more **rain** than is found in the other islands. However, the rainy days are strewn irregularly throughout the year. Most of the rain falls in December and January, when it rains on about 14 days. You must still calculate with 3 days of rain in May, while there is absolute dryness from June to August. Statistically October has 6 days of rain again, but it is not very plentiful. In the mountains, though, it can still rain in summer.

The number of **hours of sun** per day corresponds to this. In December and January the very strong winter sun shines only about 4.5 hours. Even in May the wanderer must reconcile himself to 10.1 hours of sun daily and the swimmer in August to 12.1. October is pleasant for autumn walkers once again, with 7.8 hours of sun per day.

Strong **north winds** are characteristic of the Aegean Islands, with three to four Beaufort on a yearly average. One reason for this is the air pressure difference between the Azore highs and the hot low pressure areas above the Persian Gulf. In the transition season, especially in April and May and then October and

November, the Boréas dominates, a cool, wet north wind. In the summer, mainly between May and September, the famous etesien winds, called the meltémia (from the Turkish word "meltem", the breeze) often blow for days under a cloudless blue sky, regularly strong from north to northeast, with velocities of five to six Beaufort. The sky can then be somewhat overcast. Towards evening the meltémi usually slackens somewhat, but it can also blow with quite great strength for days on end.

The schirókko occurs less frequently, but especially in the spring. It comes from the hot Sahara desert, picks up moisture over the Mediterranean to bring the Aegean warm humidity from the south.

On the Greek islands there are several different **seasons for walking tours.** Anyone wanting to give his eyes a treat should plan his tour around Easter. It might be somewhat cool and even muddy, but the countryside is grass-green, poppy-red and broom-yellow; the houses and alleyways are freshly white-washed. Even just the preparations for the Greek Easter celebration are worth the trip. However, you can't go swimming yet, and some hotels and tavernas are still closed. In April it can rain at the spur of a moment. The Greeks divide the year in three parts, and this one is called "the time blossoming and maturing".

In May and June the blossom time is already partially over, but, since it is very warm and the number of tourists is still limited, this is probably the loveliest time for walking. Beginning at the end of May the water has a pleasant temperature.

The main tourist season in July and August is not highly recommended for walking tours due to the heat. It is the "dry period" in Greece. The north winds, which blow consistently, still make the temperatures bearable, but at noon a shady spot under a tree is advisable. Harvest time begins in July. On August 15, the Assumption of the Virgin, in the eastern church called "Passing Away Peacefully", there are great celebrations everywhere with roast lamb, music and dance.

From the beginning of September on, the heat is over and the sea still has a pleasant temperature for swimming until the end of October. Now longer walking tours can be taken once again, but only until about 6 p.m. due to the shorter period of daylight. The land has become yellow and brown, the fields bear their fruit, and everywhere you meet friendly farmers harvesting their last crops. Starting at the beginning of October it can start to rain again. The restaurants and hotels gradually shut down, and some owners travel to their winter residences in Athens. Others put on camouflage suits, reach for their guns and search through the brush. A million Greeks are passionate hunters. In November there is usually a change in climate, with heavy rainfall. Then it becomes unpleasant. The period from November to February is called the "rain season". Although there are some warm, sunny days around Christmas, it is more pleasant at home.

Geology

The "Southern Sporades", to which Sámos and the islands of the Dodecanese archipelago belong, are shelf islands. They rise up to 1500 metres out of the submarine Asiatic continental base, the shelf, and were separated from the Asian continent as the geological history of the earth developed. The northern Aegean was not flooded by the sea until after the last ice age. After various actions of rising and falling, the islands took on their present form. The floor of the sea falls down to 1000 m towards the west and, where the tectonic plates meet, forms the geological border to Europe. Seaquakes occur there from time to time.

The island is about 44 km long and 19 km wide and is a blend of limestone with marble and mica-schist interstratifications. Two high mountain massifs have formed: Far to the west rises up the highest in the Aegean, the Kerkis massif (1,443 m). Towards the west the hilly country around Kondeíka forms the link with the central Ámbelos massif (1,153 m). This stretches right across the island from north to south. To the east of it is more hilly country rising up to 450 m and in-between are the only sizeable, connected plains. This is where the settlement of the island began; it now has about 34,000 inhabitants.

Fauna

Large wild animals have been exterminated here; hence, besides wild boar, large game is not encountered. Hares and martens are seldom. The animals one most often comes across are donkeys, goats and sheep, though not in such large numbers as in former years. Sometimes even pasture land is burned off, in order to create fresh nutriments for goats. The few cows have an almost exotic charm.

Of the smaller animals one hears and sees the small common lizard, which can be up to 10 cm long. The dragon-like agama (hardun) ⊡, its bigger relative, is up to 30 cm long. Even land turtles have now become rare.

The careful wanderer will rarely see snakes. There is only one poisonous type: the horn or sand viper 2. It can be up to 50 cm long and as thick as two thumbs. A healthy adult hardly need fear a deadly bite.

The non-poisonous sand-boa is about the same size. The non-poisonous four-striped-adder reaches an adult length of more than a metre and a width almost as thick as an arm. Its size is frightening, but it is harmless, as is the ring-snake. As long as one does not move completely silently, the snakes disappear again. Long trousers give additional protection. On no account should one lift up large stones, as snakes may be sleeping underneath them.

The up to 5 cm long scorpions also hide there. The bite of a scorpion is rather painful but not deadly. They also love to hide in shoes.

You can rouse crabs, frogs and eels along the watercourses. In rocky bays you should look out for sea urchins 3.

Soaring above in search of prey are birds such as buzzards, falcons and griffon vultures; unfortunately migratory birds often fall victim to the Greek passion for hunting.

4

5

6

Flora

Sámos is significantly greener and fruitful since the clouds collect in the mountains of Asia Minor and bring greater amounts of rain in winter. The **stock of trees** mostly consists of pine forests which, however, have frequently fallen victim to the flames in recent years. Taller evergreen oaks and kermes oaks ① grow in protected regions which are rich in water. Unassuming, salt-tolerant tamarisks ② are found along beaches. "Oriental strawberry trees" with red trunks ③ are also to be found. Plane-trees ④ shade the village squares and slender cypresses the cemeteries. Acacias, poplars, alders, maples and eucalyptus trees ⑤ can also be found, as well as mulberry trees ⑥ and carobs ⑦. Among the fruit trees there are pomegranates, fig trees ⑧ and citrus fruits. Yet dominating the landscape most of all is the olive tree, which looks strangely deformed as it gets older.

In the open countryside dry shrubs reaching a height of up to half a metre predominate, thorny undergrowth (garrigue) called **phrýgana** in Greek. Typical representatives of this "low mac-

7

8

9

chia" are broom, thorny knap-weed, heather, spiny spurge plants (euphorbia) 9 10, plants often shaped like hedgehogs. Jerusalem sage, squill and asphodel 11 blossom there.

Thicker bush or tree groups up to two metres high with evergreens and bushes with hard leaves are not found as frequently. This "high macchia" is called **xerovoúmi** in Greek. Kermes oaks with serrated leaves 1, juniper and mastic bushes 12 are particularly predominant.

The agave 13, attributed to the cactus family, often lines the lanes and paths. This thorny leaf plant has only grown in the Mediterranean area since the 16th century. The fruit of the fig-cactus 14 makes a sweet supplement to any hiker's picnic.

Along with Spain, Greece has the greatest variety of plants in Europe. **Flowers** can mainly be appreciated in spring. Already in January the anemone and crocus blossom. Then, from February through to May/June, all the splendour of white and red blossoming rockroses 15, iris, yellow daffodils, hyacinths, lupines, chrysanthemums and broom add magic to the landscape with

their cheery colours, and the poppy adds its bright red.

Small **orchids** are an adornment of spring for a short time. The bee orchid (ophrys) 16, lax-flowered orchid (orchis), tongue orchid (serapias) and dragon arum 17 can be seen frequently.

In May and June the main blossoming season comes to an end, but summer doesn't mean brown wilderness by any means. Bougainvillea radiates its bright colours on the house walls, and oleander blossoms in moist spots. The thorny acanthus 18 and the gold thistle 19 bloom along the wayside. When the summer heat subsides, meadow-saffron, heather and squill reveal themselves along with the dandelions, thistles and cyclamen.

Sage 20, capers 21 and other kitchen herbs often border the walking paths. While walking you can especially appreciate the pleasantly spicy aroma of thyme, rosemary, lavender, oregano, camomile and fennel. Cultivated in the coastal plains are potatoes, wheat and vegetables. And, of course the famous Samos wine.

A brief history

Prehistoric Period   In the 4th millennium BC human life establishes itself in the Kámpos plain and near Pythagório for the first time. The first immigrants, the Carians, came from Asia Minor about 5000 years ago via the Mycale Strait.

Around 1500 BC the first Minoan settlers come from Crete, from 1400 Mycenaean settlers from the Peloponnese. After 1100 BC the Aegean islands and the coast of Asia Minor are systematically colonised by peoples from the Greek mainland. The Aegean Sea becomes Greek. There are contacts to the Phoenicians, a trading and seafaring people from the coast of what is now Lebanon. They impart the skills of the Assyrians and Babylonians to the Greeks, as well as introducing writing and money.

Archaic Period   (700–490 BC) The Ionians dominate the northern Aegean; south of the island of Léros the Spartan Dorians prevail. Ionian Samos, with colonies in Asia Minor, North Africa and on the Black Sea, now flourishes and ranks among the leading city states in the Mediterranean. Its ingenious ruler Polycrates (535–522 BC) has important edifices erected. An enormous navy connects the city with the Caucasus, Egypt and Mesopotamia. Thinkers such as Pythagoras and Eupalinos live on Sámos.

Starting in 540 BC, the Persian Empire extends its influence to the coast of Asia Minor. The Greeks of the Aegean and Asia Minor together with first Sparta, later Athens, form the Athenian-Delian League. The island of Délos becomes the intellectual and cultural centre of this alliance. The Persian Wars begin in 490 BC.

The Classical Period   (490–336 BC) Sámos, Persian since 522, fights on the Persian side at the beginning of the wars, but Sámos, too, is on Athens' side for the final triumph over the Persians in 449 BC. Immense riches are amassed on Délos during the Golden Age which follows. When Athens carries off the treasure and tries to make vassals of its allies, they fight in the Peloponnesian War in alliance with Sparta against Athens. The inhabitants of Sámos also rise up against Athens and are driven off the island. This fratricidal war brings an end to the heyday of Greece, Athens losing all importance for over 2,000 years.

Hellenistic Period   (338–146 BC) The Macedonians in northern Greece take over the Greek culture after conquering Greece in

338 BC and then shortly afterwards the islands. For a short period Alexander the Great, a Macedonian, takes this culture, henceforth known as "Hellenism", as far as India. His successors, the Diadochi of the Antigonid dynasty, allow the Samians to return in 321 BC. They stimulate a second golden age in economic and intellectual terms. The astronomer Aristarchus is the first to develop the heliocentric model of the universe which we now call the "Copernican" model.

Roman Period   (146 BC–330 AD) After 146 BC the Romans, as the next rulers, also make the Greek culture their own, thus helping its spread throughout Europe. The Greek culture becomes that of the Occident. Sámos does not become Roman until 133 BC, but quickly establishes itself as the preferred winter residence of the Roman emperors. In 51 AD the apostle Paul travels through the islands, which have very early contact to Christianity, which also becomes the state religion in the Eastern Roman Empire (Byzantine Empire) in 391 AD.

The Byzantine Period   (330–1204 AD) While the Western Roman Empire is declining during the migration of peoples in 476 AD, the eastern part of the Imperium Romanum remains an upholder of Graeco-Roman culture. Byzantium, the second Rome, turns eastwards, brings Christianity to the Slavs and spreads Greek ideas as far as Moscow, which later becomes known as the Second Byzantium or Third Rome.
The new Islamic ideas also influence Greece in the 8th and 9th centuries. In the feud over pictures, iconoclasm, the admissibility of a pictorial representation of God and the Saints is disputed. Europe begins to drift apart in cultural terms; the religious differences also deepen. It is disputed whether the Holy Ghost only emanates from God the Father or also from his Son, as the Roman Catholic Church believes. Another controversy is the corporal ascension of Mary, which is considered as a "peaceful passing away" in the Orthodox Church. In 1054 the schism or final separation of the Eastern Greek-Orthodox Church from the Western Latin Church of Rome comes about.
In the "Dark Centuries" from the 7th to the 9th century the Aegean Islands are often attacked and occupied by the Vandals, Goths, Normans and then the Saracens. The inhabitants of the islands withdraw into the mountain villages and build fortresses like the Kástro Louloudás ㉕. It isn't until the 9th century that Byzantium can consolidate its power once again. Now, however,

in the wake of the Persians, Avars, Arabs and Seljuks, a new great Asian power has assembled on the eastern borders of Byzantium: the Turkish Ottoman Empire. It pushes westward with immense force. In 1095 the Eastern Roman Empire requests help from Pope Urban II, and the crusades begin. They are a fiasco. Jerusalem, which has been a place of pilgrimage until now, cannot be held on to by the Christians. During the fourth crusade, one of the most short-sighted campaigns in history is initiated: Due to trade rivalries, Venice induces the crusaders to plunder the Byzantine capital, Constantinople, in 1204. The quadriga on San Marco square is one part of the loot. Byzantium is too weak to ever recover again and is conquered by the Turks in 1453.

Venetian and Genoese Period   (1204–1470) For most of the Aegean islands the Sack of Constantinople is followed first by Venetian, then Genoese rule. Genoa owns Sámos since 1304, but is later unable to guarantee the security of the population and transfers it to the more strongly fortified island of Chios. Around 1470 Turkish troops occupy the now almost unpopulated island and name it "Sisam adasi".
After Constantinople falls in 1453 and Rhodes in 1523, the Turks push further west. Not until Vienna and Lepanto can the Pope's "Holy league" halt their triumphal march.

The Turkish Era   (1470–1912) The Fall of Constantinople in 1453 marks the end of the thousand-year-old advanced Greek civilisation. Learned Byzantine fugitives bring the Greek way of thinking back to the West once again, paving the way for the Renaissance. From this time on, the fortune of the Orthodox Church is determined in Moscow, which also assumes the Byzantine double-headed eagle and the Roman Imperial claim for power. Pan-Slavism under Catherine the Great seeks to bring the Balkan Slavs into the Russian fold. The Turkish-Russian war extends as far as the Aegean, where a Russian fleet occupies Sámos from 1771–74; it later returns to Turkish rule.
Yet the whole of Greek life, from music to diet, is dominated by Turkish influence for the next 350 years. This influence is still recognisable to a degree today. There is somewhat greater freedom on the islands, but this always depends on the current representative of the "Sublime Porte" in Istanbul. The Orthodox Church proves to be the safeguard of Greek culture. Children are taught the Greek language and writing in secret schools. The head of the church remains – then also as guarantor of the submissiveness of

the Greeks – in Istanbul, to this day. When unrest breaks out in 1821, the Patriarch of the time is executed.

Independent Greece   (since 1830) At the beginning of the 19th century, Europe reflects on its cultural roots. Philhellenists from many countries support the Greek struggle for independence after 1821, the Great Powers in Europe help diplomatically, and Greece becomes a part of Europe again.

However, not the islands in front of the Turkish coast. The London Protocol of 1830 regulates the new order in the Aegean area and determines their continued dependence on Turkey. Only Sámos gets greater autonomy in administration.

Twentieth Century   The kingdom of Greece tries to regain possession of its former settlements from the "sick man on the Bosporus". During the 1912–13 Balkan Wars and the First World War several islands and Ottoman areas on the northern coast of the Aegean are occupied. After the First World War, among whose losers is Turkey, the Greeks start a war over the former areas in Asia Minor. But Turkey, emboldened once again by the "Young Turk Revolution", utterly destroys the Greeks in 1922, who then have to agree to a major population exchange. Many of them end up on Sámos which, on account of forfeiting its trade links with the mainland, falls into a deep economic crisis.

After 1936 Greece goes through a military dictatorship. In October 1940 Mussolini attacks the country. When the Italians are pushed back, Hitler orders the country to be taken and hands it over to Italy and Bulgaria as an occupation zone. After Mussolini's fall in 1943 British and Greek troops occupy Sámos, but the island is reconquered by German troops until October 1944.

After World War II   With Western help during the civil war from 1945 to 1949, Greece avoids the fate of the other Balkan countries, and doesn't disappear behind the Iron Curtain. It is accepted by the European Union, whose subsidies for improving the infrastructure and developing tourism become the most important sector of the economy. In 2002, the drachma, the oldest currency in the world, is replaced by the euro. The new, "hard" currency gives Greece easier access to financial resources, which many politicians are unable to resist. Unnoticed, huge mountains of debt are accumulated, which are used to service widespread clientelism. In 2009 this leads Greece and Europe into the worst crisis of the post-war period.

❶ High above the Bay of Vathí

The five to six-hour trek mainly takes country lanes.
From the peak of Profítis Elías one enjoys the view
across the Bay of Vathí before walking, partly be-
neath shady trees, round Mount Thios. In Kamára a
spring and a taverna provide refreshment.
■ *12 km, difference in altitude 320 m, moderate*

AWT 0.00	At the **ferry terminal of Sámos** go to the right of the classicist building with the shipping agencies into the narrow covered alley, bear left after the steps and go round the church in a right-hand arc. The "Street of the
0.05	28th October" climbs up to the **sports stadium.** 80 m behind it, where the street bends to the left, take the concrete track up right. After 30 m, in front of dwellings, turn
0.10	up left and pass a tiled **chapel** (right) in what is here already a rural environment. 100 m after crossing the bypass, you see a little house with cypress on the right after a left bend. Behind it turn right at the electricity meter
!!	(**P1:** N37°45.752'/E26°58.507') into the garden, *after 5 m*
!!	left and *immediately right again* on to a marked path. This climbs through bushes and ends on a roadway, which you take to the left. After 200 m you discover *above on the left*
0.20	a white **stone cross** ①. Here you climb left across a few rocks and notice a derelict house on the right.
	The occasionally rather overgrown path first leads through pines, then runs above an olive grove (left) and below terraced vineyards. Where these end (**P2:** N37°45.901'/E26°58.645') you ascend the line of slope to
0.25	the **roadway.** With a splendid view of the bay you keep

0.40   climbing left for 15 minutes until you reach a **fork.**

    Short cut: If you want to return to the town from here, take the roadway running downhill and, 10 m before the next fork, the path going down left. At the bottom, again on the roadway, you wander left downhill, past the Panteleimon Chapel (right), **back to Vathí** in altogether 40 minutes.

0.40   From the **fork** a rocky path on the right leads after 10 m up between two pines. White-washed stones facilitate ori-
0.50   entation, past a stone tower, as far the **Chapel of the Prophet Elías** (320 m). You can survey the enormous bay with the north coast and regain your breath for the way ahead.

    In front of the aerials you then go left down a roadway,
!!   but *straight ahead* on to a short-cut path in the first *left-*
0.55   *hand bend.* At the bottom this path joins a **roadway** (P3:
1.00   N37°46.191′/E26°58.684′), which first leads across a **ridge,**
1.05   then to a round **reservoir** (right).

    Alternative: 20 m further several *indistinct trails* run left down into the forest, where orientation becomes easier. At the end of the forest path you come to a fork (AWT 1.15).

| 1.05 | Staying on the wide descending roadway, you reach a |
| 1.15 | **fork** and march right down into the Arkoudólaka plateau. (One could leave the roadway after 80 m and take a path ② on the right, which however later becomes indistinct. Finally one drops steeply down to the roadway.) |

The roadway leads past a farmhouse (left). Later you can shorten a bend by walking through an olive grove. Beneath shady olive trees one thirstily trundles along the edge of the fertile plain ③, later descending right to the gi-

| 1.50 | ant **plane-tree of Kamára**, where fresh spring water bur- bles – further down in taverna "Kriton" alfa beer swishes into the glasses. |

In front of the taverna you take the road along the Vla-marí plateau, going right over a hilltop where another

2.10	road **merges** and downhill again beyond the turning to Vathí.
2.15	60 m beyond that you stroll along the old **kalderími**, past the Dimítros Chapel (left) ④. Despite damage caused by road construction, the track is passable and is being re-paired. Further down you traverse the by-pass diagonally. On the paved path which follows you touch the road and, after 10 m, drop left down the old paving stones to
2.25	**Sámos**. Next to a plane-tree is the chicken inn "Kotópoula", which can be recommended. Continue in
2.35	this direction as far as the **shore road.**

❷ The chapel in the forest

Besides the two large convents Ayía Zóni and Zoo-dóchos Pigí the small Giannis chapel is one of the destinations on the five to six-hour trek. It runs along rural lanes, an old kalderími and forest paths. At the end it follows little side roads for half an hour. In Kamára is a welcoming taverna, in the convents are wells. The higher of the two convents already closes its doors at 13.30 hours!

■ *18 km, diff. in altitude 330 m, moderate to difficult*

AWT   For about eight euro a taxi will drop you off comfortably at the convent **Ayía Zóni** (Holy Girdle) – the first 125 metres in altitude are accomplished! The harmonious inner courtyard from 1695 and the church with its wonderful 18th century frescoes are accessible again following renovation.

0.00   In front of the **side with the entrance** to the convent you slowly descend the little road and, after 100 m, go
0.05   right at the first junction. At the following **T-junction** you first go 20m to the right, then left on to an initially ascending rural lane, with a shed on the right. Above the rock face to the far right waits the first destination ①. Disregard a few left turns – but not the one that comes after four minutes, where the main track climbs slightly (**P1:** N37°45.222'/E27°00.857'). Here you go down left and, after 100m, at a garden gate (left), up right along a wide stony swath and then down to a roadway.

     This takes you left through a dip, then straight ahead up-
0.15   hill, likewise at a **right turn.** The path later has a concrete

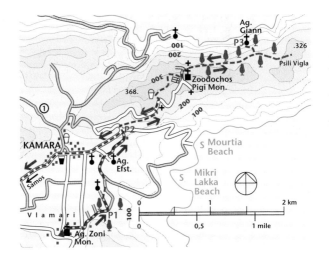

surface and crosses a concrete track at a house (left). (The chapel Áyios Efstáthios stays to your right.) Straight ahead you proceed along a roadway, past two deserted military

0.25 barracks (right), as far as a **road junction** (**P2:** N37° 45.769'/E27°01.008).

Go up the road for 100m, but then right at the left-hand bend into the shady kalderími! After about ten minutes it rejoins the road, which you take uphill for 200 m. At a

0.40 right-hand bend more **steps** begin on the left, leading to a (dry) well house and then to the continuation of the kalderími ②. Soon the convent comes into view. Along-

0.50 side the cemetery (right) you reach the gate of the **convent Zoodóchos Pigí** (life-giving spring). Hopefully you make it before 13.30 hours.

> The oldest parts of the convent date back to 1756. The central cruciform domed basilica is supported by four ancient columns from Milet. However the local visitors are more interested in the icon of the Virgin Mary.
>
> From the monument standing in front of the convent you can look down at the 1.2 km wide strait of Mycale, scene of two naval battles, in which the Greeks defeated the Persians in 479 BC and the Turkish-Egyptian fleet in 1824. Nowadays a focal point for illegal immigration to the EU.

Above the convent a concrete track laid by the military

leads you on – but where it makes a left-hand bend, you set off on your own roadway to the right. The roadway ends 30 m to the right of a three metre tall shrine (330 m). Here, in the continuation, you walk on into a sparse pine forest . A stone pyramid with the inscription "Ag. Giannaki" (right) points the way there. The path runs through waist-high bushes to a **left turn** *at right angles*. There you descend on to a narrow forest path, but taking care to remember *the way back*.

!!
1.05
!!

After seven minutes you suddenly stand in front of the **Giannis Chapel** made of rough stone  (**P3:** N37°46.374'/ E27°02.425', 220 m). Inside it has little to offer, but its concealed location is spectacular. The only trouble is that you have to find your way back and regain the 110 metres difference in altitude! Once back on the **main path**, you go to the right back to the tall **shrine**.

★
1.20
1.35

From there you follow the same route back: From the convent along the kalderími past the small cemetery (left) and later down **steps** to the road, where you turn right and descend the steps on the left and proceed to the continuation of the kalderími.

1.50

On the **road** you first go down left for 100m, but right at the already familiar junction as far as **Kamára.** There you can, depending on your needs, take a cool beer in the "Kriton" or fresh spring water at the well above it.

2.00
2.10

From here you follow the description for ① as far as **Sámos harbour.**

2.50

❸ Beneath the Ámpelos Mountains

On this walk you proceed from Mytiliní to Kokkári in four hours. For the most part you wander along country lanes; only the last stretch leads along narrow forest paths. You will not face any great ascents or orientation problems. A stop for refreshment can be taken at the beginning and at the end of this walk, which is especially lovely in its final section.
■ *11 km, diff. in altitude 225 m, easy to moderate*

The palaeontological museum in Mytiliní is 800 m up the hill and presents preserved specimens of animals found in the area and an interesting seismic map.

AWT 0.00 — At the **Platía in Mytiliní** you could enjoy a frappé – as a trekker in the café "Kalderími", of course. From there you walk down to the left along the street going towards Sámos town. After 50 m you turn left at the signpost to Kokkári 🚏 and pass a church (right). At the next junction you bear right into the *Odos Aristarchou*, then past another church (right) into winding *Nikitara Street* and out of the village. Up on the left beyond a car park stands a

0.05 — **chapel** which gives us its blessings as we set off. Go straight ahead at the signposts and, at the fork with the concrete block, up left.

For quite a while you then stay on the same level as you traverse the zone burnt by the fires of 2000 (left). Standing up on the hill to the right is a dilapidated windmill.

0.20 — After going over a hill, the track **forks** (**P1:** 37°44.175'/ E26°53.757', 190 m).

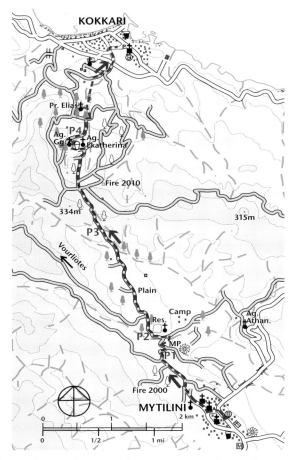

You go down a few meanders to a rest area, from where a restored monopáti leads through a shady valley and up the other side to a country lane, which you take to the left. At the sign go up right, with the **reservoir (P2: N37°44.393'/E26°53.738')** on the right. After that you amble down through a wooded area into a wide hollow. At the turn-off to Vourliótes, walk straight on and disregard any further turn-offs to the left. The path leads to the left and then a bit uphill above a hollow. Stay to the right at a fork and you will come to a **small ravine (P3: N37°**

45.057'/E26°53.335') running diagonally to the lane. Even in summer there is water here.

Afterwards you proceed uphill through a burnt pine wood
1.00 above a ravine and come to a fork with a **view of the sea** (225 m.), the highest point along this walk. Here it is possible to appreciate the full extent of the 2010 forest fire, which was deliberately caused as a result of a family feud. Exactly on the opposite side you stroll light-footedly downhill and then straight on at the turn-off to the right which appears shortly afterwards. Pass by the next turn-off to the left, but shortly afterwards there is a sharp-an-
!! gled turn-off to the left which you should follow. Soon
1.10 you will discover the **Chapel to Saint Catherine** ②. This shady rest area with a fountain will do you good now.

Along a narrow path you pass the fountain (left) and wander through a shady hollow and up again. Where a path turns off to the left, continue straight on and you will
1.15 come to a dusty white **dirt road** (**P4:** N37°45.925'/E26°53.167') which you should entrust yourself to, walking downhill to the right. After four minutes, in a curve to the
!! right, there is a *cairn* on the left announcing a short nar-
1.20 row **forest path** to the left. Shortly afterwards you come
!! to the dusty road once again and discover *another cairn* on the right of the next junction, this one announcing a true jungle path ③. The completely covered path leads downhill, then through a stream-bed and finally ends in a dirt road going downhill to the right. Behind a chicken coop
1.30 (left), walk to the right into a **hollow lane** and to the main by-passing street. On the other side of this street is
1.45 the beginning of a footpath to the **church in Kokkári** ④. From here it is only another few metres to the seafront.

❹ Water for Pythagório

The Eupalinos Tunnel is one of the masterpieces of ancient engineering skill. Every visitor to Sámos knows this water passageway's outlet. After this four-hour circular walk, you will know where the water was conducted from. In addition you wander past a lovely monastery and discover springs, but no tavernas.
Having started off in the forest, the trail mostly follows roadways.

■ *10 km, difference in altitude 190 m, moderate*

AWT   Between Pythagório and Sámos Town is the **bus stop Mesokámbos** (with Jet petrol station). From it you drop 100 m to the "Sidero Jefiraki", the former "iron bridge", now made of concrete.

0.00   Behind the bridge is the factory for **Samos Ouzo.** Since it is still too early for a tasting session, take the dirt road to the right (on the left of the supermarket) and walk uphill at the fork after 5 minutes. The leisurely walk along the edge of a pine forest and a fertile valley is very pleasant. The

0.15   small **chapel** of Saint Panteleimon later appears up on the left between olive trees. Later you discover two-storey high

0.20   **ruins with cypress trees** ① on the left. Two minutes (or
!!   200 m) later, turn off *to the left at a sharp angle* and continue uphill. (Opposite the turn-off a concealed dirt road leads down into the valley.) Later you see the wind rotors

0.25   on the hill and pass by a **stream-bed.**

Disregard two turn-offs to the left. Shortly after a turn-off to the right a 50 m long path leads to the left into the

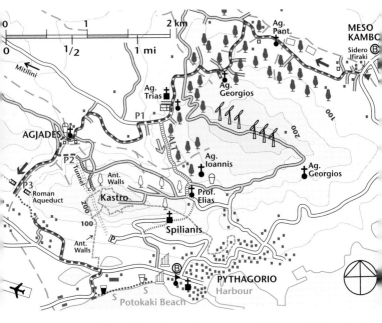

0.30 woods, and directly to the romantically located **chapel of St. George.**

After it the road ascends more steeply and leads past a
0.40 meadow (left) to a **T-junction.** Turn left here and walk through a furrow in the terrain. Continue straight on, with a lovely view of the broad Mytiliní valley, until you
0.45 reach the nunnery **Moní Ayías Triádas** ②.

The living quarters, built in 1924, form a shady quadratic courtyard, in the middle of which the Katholikón, constructed in 1905, arises. The picturesque construction can be visited from 8:00 am –1:00 pm and from 4:00 pm – 8:00 pm.

Continue downhill along the asphalt road in a wide curve to the right.

Alternative: You can reach the chapel of Profítis Elías along the street running up left and from there wander uphill to the **ancient city walls.** On the way down you pass the **Spilianís Monastery** and return to **Pythagório** after a total of three hours.

0.50 At the second **turn-off (P1:** N37°42.397′/ E26°56.117′)

you go left on to a country lane. On the left you see the mountain ridge which was scorched in the fire of 2000, crowned by the remains of the mighty walls of the ancient city of Pythagório. Walk between fields of corn and vineyards until you come to a **T-junction**, where you turn to the left and then at the next fork to the right to reach the semi-derelict hamlet of **Agiádes.**

1.05

1.10

> *The ancient spring house is still hidden directly below the church of Áyos Ioánnis. Water from the plains was collected there. From the south side of the present-day church a hidden passage conducted the water 800 m to the entrance of the tunnel.*
>
> *Today the water is transported to Pythagório in pipes.*

In Agiádes you cross over the ford, turn to the left after 20 m – still *between the houses* – on to a path and then continue uphill to the right until you reach a **dirt road.** Walk down it to the left for *200 steps* (= 2 minutes) into a valley. When you see excavated cliffs on the right and discover a metal bracket on the ground, turn left on to a narrow footpath leading downhill. Having traversed the sometimes overgrown stream-bed and walked uphill for 80 m, you come to the scorched area of woods. In front of a few tree trunks lying on the ground, walk uphill to the right without a path. Five metres before reaching the hill-top you climb over a tree trunk on the left and, behind it, find a path which, after 50 metres, runs horizontally to the newly bricked, closed entrance of the **Eupalinos Tunnel** ③ (**P2:** N37°42.185′/E26°55.512′) .

1.15

!!

1.20

> *The tunnel is one of the most grandiose ancient constructions from the middle of the 6th century BC. In order to be able to supply the 20,000 inhabitants of the*

city of Pythagório with water, even in times of siege, the tyrant Polycrates (p. 33) gave the architect Eupalinos the task of planning a tunnel 1036 m long. Its construction was begun simultaneously from both sides. The height of each entrance was set by determining a level area around the mountain. When the northern section was dug out, the direction had to be changed several times due to mining problems. The connection of the two sections was planned exactly under the peak, and this connection of the paths was actually accomplished by means of semicircular surveying arches.

To transport the water, a ditch was then dug into the incline next to the path, 1.0 m to 8.50 m lower. Later, pipes made of clay were embedded.

In the period of rough construction, which lasted from eight to ten years, 7000 cbm of rubble had to be removed from the tunnel, where only two men at a time could work with hammer and chisel.

After the tunnel had been used for supplying water for 1000 years, it was forgotten and wasn't rediscovered until 1881. From 1959 on it was researched in more detail by German and Greek archaeologists.

Alternative: From the tunnel, you could continue by walking uphill to a road, through the scorched tree trunks and over **Mount Kástro** with its fortified walls.

1.20 Otherwise, return to the road from the **tunnel**, walking through the stream-bed again and turning downhill to the left on the road in the gorge there. You can soon see

1.35 the **arches of an aqueduct** ④ (**P3:** N 37°42.042'/E26° 55.152').

The precisely constructed brick arches indicate immediately that this is a Roman structure. The water from the Eupalinos Tunnel was insufficient for the Romans with their extravagant bathing culture, so additional water had to be conducted in open canals along the slopes from the area around Milí.

100 m after the aqueduct you leave the dirt road and climb to the left up the hill. On top of it you come – at first without a path – to a lane, then to a little road. From

1.55 there you descend to the **main road** and later reach the

2.05 **beach of Potokáki** with its kiosks and bars. You don't have to just drink water any more.

The Tyrant of Sámos

The highlight of the history of Sámos was 2,600 years ago. Under its ruler Polycrates the light of Greek Antiquity is kindled here, in Chíos and above all in Milet.

The islands of the Aegean and the surrounding coastal areas have been settled by Greeks since as early as 1,000 BC. The Ionians gain a foothold in the middle zone, from Attica through the Cyclades to the Asian mainland around Milet. This most creative of all Greek tribes develops unimaginably new things in the spheres of politics, trade, architecture, philosophy, astronomy and poetry. It also benefits from the contact with the Phoenicians. This trading and seafaring people from the coast of what is today Lebanon transfers the knowledge of Mesopotamia.

Fertile Sámos has a special role. Around 538 BC the patrician Polycrates seizes power here. Having eliminated his brothers, who had initially reigned with him, he rules the island as a tyrant. Originally this meant "absolute ruler", but his unscrupulousness discredits the concept for all time. He crushes all resistance and, through the raids of his powerful fleet, amasses unheard-of riches. Samian colonies arise throughout the Mediterranean and Black Sea regions. For a while a military alliance connects him with Egypt.

His urge to build knows no boundaries either: The gigantic city walls and the harbour jetty of Pythagório, the unfinished Temple of Hera and the Eupalinos Tunnel are still famous today. The great minds of those days gather at his court, among them the genius Samian philosopher and mathematician Pythagoras. But he quarrels with the tyrant and flees. The historian Herodot recorded this, as well as the fall of Polycrates: In 522 BC the Persian governor invites him over to promising negotiations on the mainland, only to have him murdered. His corpse is put on display on the opposite shore. His legendary fortune had deserted him.

Sámos then becomes the first Greek island to fall under the influence of Persia. But the Ionian spirit wanders further to Athens where, 100 years later, Ancient Greece bursts into bloom.

❺ The Temple of Hera

*The destinations on this four to five-hour walk are
two important monuments. First you visit the no-
table fortified monastery of The Mother of God,
Moní tis Megális Panagías. Old frescoes can be mar-
velled at there (closed Tuesdays).*
*Then you walk down along old, hardly known paths
to reach the fertile coastal plains and a pretty rural
village. The remains of the Heraíon, the largest
Greek temple ever planned, await you at the end of
the walk (closed Mondays and from 3:00 p.m. on!) It
is easiest to reach the starting point by taxi.*
■ *10 km, difference in altitude 310 m, easy*

AWT
0.00   On the southern edge of the mountain village of
Koumaradéi a cement path on the right of a **small
church** ① leads downhill and past a small cemetery
(right), then to the right in a serpentine curve and after
0.06   that straight on at the **fork to the left.** The scars created
by the great forest fires have mostly healed – a pine forest
stood here in 1993. After a left-hand bend you enter a hol-
0.15   low where the inventory fit for a museum is slowly turning to rust in the ruins of a **mill.** Behind it, our road leads
around a hill and on uphill to the Byzantine monastery of
0.25   Moní tis **Megális Panagías** ②, which proudly awaits your
visit – but only until 1:00 p.m.

*The Katholikón, the cruciform-domed church in the mid-
dle built in 1593, is surrounded by four elongated residential buildings which have arrow-slit like windows on
the exterior. In the 17th century about 70 monks lived be-*

hind the picturesque arcades. After a fire in 1988 renovations were made, and 3 monks now live here once again. They sell a good description of the monastery.

★ *In the vestibule of the church, the Nartex, frescoes from the 16ᵗʰ century lead the visitor from the day of the Last Judgement back to the expulsion from Paradise. A river of fire streams from the throne and drags the sinners into Hell.*

In the main room there is the iconostasis from 1740 and a high-quality marble floor (Adam and Eve). All the walls are covered with frescoes which are, however, very darkened. Above the entrance there is the Passing Away of Maria and beneath it on the right the Archangel Michael.

Our continuation begins 15 m left of the upper access into the main street. Left of the little wall along the street ③ (**P1:** N37°41.685'/E26°50.632') you turn downhill into the terrain, wander past a bush on your left and look for the remains of the path leading along the hill and on

0.45 down to the sea and the plains. Once there, follow a **dirt road** after a fence (right) to the right. After wandering through farmland which is recovering after the fire in the

1.00 year 2000, you arrive in **Míli.** Awaiting you in the church

★ square are tables in the shade and the innkeepers Fotini and Maria. It is hard having to disappoint one of them ... Afterwards you continue downhill along the lane in front of the church and turn to the right down at the bottom. Walk past the sports area and four minutes later you reach a workshop (right) where there is a fork in the road. Turn

!! to the left here, twice cross a stream-bed and, *100 m beyond the second crossing,* look for an indistinct turn-off to the left (**P2:** N37°40.656'/E26°51.217'). At first almost without a path, this runs wonderfully through the cliffs above a ravine and then into ancient olive groves, where you either keep to the right or straight on and soon reach

1.25 a **crossroads.**

Cross the street running horizontally, take the ascending concrete road lined with bushes, walk to the right in front of the well protected Swedish enclave and then down across terraces without a path until you come to an old chapel with a stonework roof.

Walk to the right along the dirt road beneath the chapel to reach the street and turn to the left there. Cross the

1.35 fields on the left to arrive at the **double chapel** of Ay.

Ioánnou & Geórgios with an altar made of an ancient pillar. Next door is the Sarakiní-Pírgos ④, named after a Greek captain in the Ottoman fleet who enjoyed life on land here. This type of building is only found in the Cyclades otherwise.

Walking along a short avenue lined by trees, you leave the quiet courtyard and then continue to the left on a dirt road until you come to a stream-bed and walk to the right along it or in it towards the sea. After about 400 m a dirt road begins on the left side of the stream. Follow it until you come to a road bridge. Cross under it and turn up left immediately, but leave the road again after only 20 m and follow a dirt road leading to the sea. At the ruins of a bunker you walk away from the sea towards the fenced-in area of the **Heraíon** which surrounds a pillar, now placed upright once again and hence visible from afar.

2.00

> *There are leaflets about the excavations in the kiosk and descriptions on the property. German archaeologists have played a leading role in the excavations since 1910.*
>
> *The findings date back to the 3rd millennium before Christ. In the first millennium BC several altars dedicated to the nature goddess Hera were built here. The golden age in the 5th century BC brought forth the Rhoikus Altar, which was only surpassed in splendour by the Pergamon Altar in the Hellenic Age. The Hera Temple III, designed by the genial architect Rhoikus, was later carried away by the tyrant Polycrates and plans were made to reconstruct it. This Hera Temple IV, which was supposed to exceed all imaginable dimensions, remained uncompleted, however. The swampy terrain was not capable of bearing a massive structure of such dimensions.*

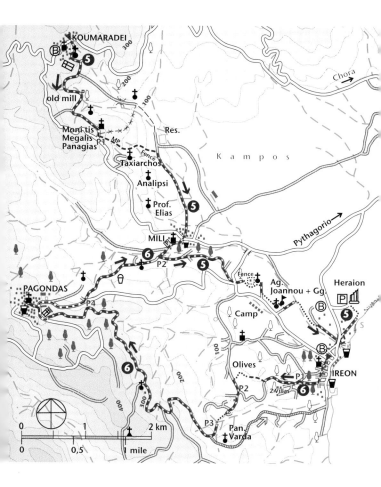

In the 5th century AD the "heathen" edifices were then used as a quarry for the construction of the early Christian basilica. Even earlier the Romans had already helped themselves when building their thermal baths. Recycling is probably the word for that nowadays.

Along the main street you will find a bus stop for the return trip to Pythagório.

⑥ Above the Kámpos Plains

The Kámpos Plains are located to the south of Pythagório. On this four to five-hour hike between Iréon and Míli you can view them from above. The rather long trek with a drawn-out ascent can be shortened. Two lovely village squares invite you to take a rest, and there are old olive groves to delight the eye.

■ *20 km, diff. in altitude 275 m, moderate to difficult*

▷ *Map see previous page*

AWT

0.00

In Iréon you walk southwards along the second street parallel to the sea, pass the church (right) and at the edge of town turn to the right **two crossings** before the pension "Ermioni". This dirt road leads through a shady little forest with a basketball court.

Beyond it tree trunks lying on the ground are a reminder of the earlier forest, which fell victim to the terrible forest fire in 2000 ①. Then two dry winters one after another, heat, negligence with fire and a storm that lasted days devastated the countryside from here all the way across to the northern coast. During the fire the olive trees were less endangered than the pines, which burned more easily due to their resin.

0.05

Walk straight up until, after a left turn-off, a **dirt road crosses** (**P1:** N37°39.681′/E26°52.622′). There you continue climbing gently, go straight ahead at two forks and up a concrete track. Standing on the hill to your left are two villas.

0.10 In a left-hand bend a **path** leads to the right away from the concrete track. After this you can master the slope in the olive grove easily without a path to reach a dirt road (**P2:** 37°39.597'/E26°52.322', 170m) at the top. Follow it to the left.

0.15 The dirt road **forks** above the next valley – you should walk to the right on level vehicle tracks, with the blue roof of the Panagía Chapel ② as your destination. Passing a right turn-off and below the wall of an olive grove, you reach a fork after seven minutes. Here you go down left and, in the next sharp left-hand bend, straight ahead without a path. Later you amble gently down through olive groves without a path and come to a small ravine. About 60 m above a circular olive grove you cross it on a path through bushes (**P3:** N37°39.361'/E26°51.864'). A

0.35 narrow **roadway** leads up left behind the bushes to the wider roadway.

> *Walk to the left to the little church **Panagía Várda**, your point of orientation. It seems to be quite old and is furnished in a humble rustic style.*

> **Short cut:** From here one could take the roadway back down to the sea.

Continue uphill to the right rather steeply and tiringly through more olive groves. Beneath you the great coastal plains stretch out – the Kámpos – where the airport is located. Pythagório is beyond this. After a house (above on

0.55 the left,) you come to a **dirt road** at the top and follow it to the right 100 m on the same level until you reach a fork with signs. Walk to the right here, too. The plains can be viewed in full now from 275 m above sea level. Sheltered from the north winds by a mountain range and irrigated by it, the Kámpos plains have been continuously inhabited by man since the Bronze Age. The proximity to Turkey is the most impressive aspect – 1.2 km. Except for at the Bosporus, there is no place else where Europe is so close to the continent of Asia. Today it is a focal point of illegal immigration to Europe.

1.10 Meanwhile a **chapel** has appeared on the left of the path near a few houses; later ancient olive trees give the wan-

1.40 derer shade. After turning inland, you get a full **view** of Pagóndas ③, spread out before you like an amphitheatre. Shrivelled olive trees border the rest of the way to the main road. Go right there and up to the wonderfully

2.00 shady platía in **Pagóndas**, where friendly proprietresses will take good care of you. Otherwise the place has nothing to offer in the way of sights.

You stroll down the village past the church (left) to the

2.05 street, which you march down smartly past a small **factory** at the edge of the village with a water basin (left). After

2.15 about a quarter of an hour **two dirt roads** turn off to the left simultaneously ④ (**P4:** N37°40.376'/E26°50.529'). Take the road leading further out of the valley and later

2.30 proceed straight on between a **chapel** and a house (*don't* turn off to the left before this).

!! Further down in the valley, *50 m before a stream-bed,* comes an indistinct fork on the right, where you could turn off to the right and reach Iréon with ⑤ in 40 min.

Míli has already appeared between the trees and looks enticing. You cross the said stream-bed and later a concreted

2.40 ford, before you arrive at the charming platía in **Míli** and can relax and stretch out your feet.

If you do not want to hoof it back to Iréon (see above, ⑤), you just have to call a taxi. Take your time; enjoy the village square first.

▷ The hotel "Samaina" in Pythagório is very popular with independent travellers. Nearly all the rooms have a view of the harbour. Tel 0030-22730-61024, www.samaina.gr

❼ Marathókampos

This village consists of three settlements: up on the slope lies the main part Marathókampos, down on the coast "Kámpos" (or "Votsalákia") and the fishing harbour "Órmos". We begin our sightseeing tour in "Kámpos", the fields. As these never used to produce great yields, they were bequeathed to the younger children. Their descendants are now very pleased with the arrangement – they are the present-day hotel owners. One of them called his restaurant "Votsalákia – pebbles", which has since become the name of this part of the village.
The three-hour trek leads along rural lanes through a bucolic landscape dominated by olive cultivation. Although almost no shade, the route does have springs and, in the villages, tavernas.
■ 8 km, difference in altitude 260 m, easy

AWT In **Votsalákia/Kámpos** take the street running uphill
0.00 from the taxi rank and, after 150 m, pass the pension
     "Magda" (p. 47). At the side street turn off left and, short-
0.05 ly afterwards, right at the **fork**, direction "Kastro Village".
     At the roundabout with the olive tree in the centre, turn
     off right and cross the "Villa Jota" on the way up.
     At the fork further up proceed straight on up. Where the
     concrete surface finishes, an overgrown kalderími branch-
     es off into the valley – but we keep going uphill. Further
     up we discover, only at second glance, the barrel-vaulted
0.15 **St. George's Chapel** on the right – but it is closed any-
     way. 200 m further on (**P1:** N 37°42.974'/E 26°40.387',

42

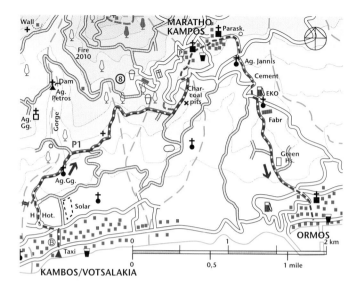

KAMBOS/VOTSALÁKIA

105 m) tracks on the left lead to a mill in the ravine ①.
Continue on the same level. Soon becoming visible are
the paving stones of the former kalderími, which our lane

0.25 now covers. Where a lane **joins** our lane from the right,
continue straight ahead, ascending gently, later passing a
blue wayside altar (left). In a green rocky gully you tra-

0.30 verse a **ford** and are surrounded by the remains of the fire
in 2010. In the next gully is a well ②. After a right turn-off
you encounter a T-junction and now see Marathókampos.
Here you go left and past a charcoal works (right). In a dip

0.45 another **charcoal-burner** plies his sooty trade. Having
crossed the road running left, you walk up the concrete

0.55 ramps as far as the domed church of **Marathókampos**
(260 m). The 400-year old mountain village has become
affluent through olive cultivation. Strolling up and down
the old alleys and steps, it is not long before you find a
wonderful well and a few inns.

From the rear side of the big church you go downhill,
keeping left in the maze of alleys. Since the church we are
looking for does not have a clearly visible dome, it is best

1.00 to ask for directions to the **Ayía Paraskeví**.

Below it we amble down the concrete track between gar-

dens, pass an overgrown watermill (left) and cross the
1.05 **road.** Standing on the other side, pointing the way, is the
Jannis Chapel (right). At a cement factory (right) we meet
!!   the road again and go downhill here – but *40 m after the
right bend* left on to a short-cut concrete track down to the
1.10 **EKO petrol station.**
Continue down the road shortly and, directly in front of
the wood factory (with chapel), down right on to a
kalderími – or rather on to what remains of it. Having
1.20 passed a run-down **greenhouse**, head towards the sea
through olive groves ③ until you catch sight of the har-
1.30 bour ④. In a jiffy you are in **Órmos Marathokámpou.**
The former fishing village now boasts quite a few attrac-
tive harbour tavernas, where you can unwind after the
hike alongside tossing fishing boats.

44

⑧ The Cave of Pythagoras

This four-hour walk on dirt roads leads from Mara-thókampos along a panoramic path to the "cave of Pythagoras" and from there down to Votsalákia.
Along the way are springs and in season the snack-bar next to the cave is open for business.
Take along electric torches for the cave!
It is also possible to take a three-hour circular walk to the monastery Áyios Geórgios.

■ *10 km, difference in altitude 370 m, moderate*

AWT 0.00
0.05
0.10

At the parking area in the lower part of **Marathókampos** (260 m) a concrete path with a large **sign** "Cave of Pythagoras" leads slightly uphill away from the main street, first past the **cemetery** (left) and then down past a small **factory** and a fountain. The dirt road follows the contours of the slope in the direction of the Kérkis Mountains. You can see the coastline with the fishing villages of Ormos Marathókampos and the bathing resort of Vot-salákia. The island of Foúrni lies in the sea mist.

0.20

The path then bears to the right and leads past the **fork** down to holiday homes (the end of the circular walk, see below). Almost following the contour lines it circles a wide valley where the chapel to Saint Peter is enthroned on a cliff ①. In the middle of the valley you can find a small **waterfall** along with water holes to romp in.

0.35

0.55

As you continue along the way, a domed church just below the path will stir your interest. After a small spring (right) is a **left turn-off** about *20 m beyond a barn* (left).

Circular walk: The half-ruined **Georgios monastery**, a

walled-in fortification monastery, is eight minutes downhill. Another ten minutes later you arrive at the chapel Ayios Petros perched on the steep rock. After this, you cross through a dry stream-bed, walk uphill and come to the original roadway again behind the holiday homes. You will return to Marathókampos in an hour AWT.

0.55   If you wander **straight** on from the left turn-off along the roadway on top towards the west, you see the massive Kérkis Mountains. Bear left at the fork (370 m) and then walk down into the valley. Soon the day's destination can be seen on the cliff opposite you: two chapels ②. You can

1.10   climb up to them from the **valley floor** (with snack-bar).

*The **Chapel to Mary**, Panagía Sarantaskaliótissa, can be reached in eight minutes, at the end up the 40 (+3) stone steps which gave the chapel its name. It is built into a cave where the genius Pythagoras is said to have fled for a short time around 530 BC after he had fallen into Polycrates' disgrace (p. 33). At the bottom of the larger cave is a spring.*

★   *This is one of the places you can only find in Greece which have always attracted hermits. Secluded in the solitude of the mountains, between heaven and earth, with commanding views of land and sea.*

1.30   Back in the **valley floor**, wander out of the valley between rocks, fields and olive trees – at first on a concrete

1.45   track. At the **turn-off** to the Evangelístra Monastery turn

1.50   down left into a little road and past a **group of houses** to the sea.

2.05   At the edge of **Votsalákia** is the nice taverna "Vangélis", where you can relax beneath shady tamarisks and have a swim.

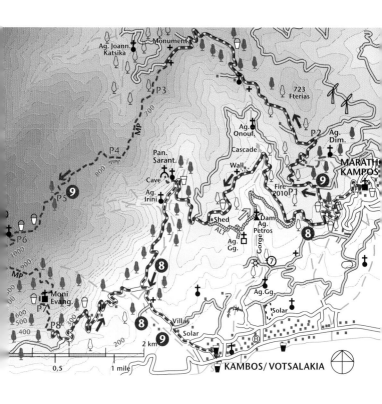

▷ Those who can dispense with a sea view in the pretty beach resort of Votsálakia may like to try the pension *Magda* with spacious apartments in a tranquil olive garden. It is 100 metres inland from the taxi rank.
Tel. 22730-37650, mob. 6974-121884,
magdalog@yahoo.gr.

▷ **Enjoy typical Greek cuisine!**
In *Anna* at the northern end of Votsalákia guests can choose their dishes from the display like in the old days. In the beach taverna *To pigádi* (well) diners sit at painted tables and chairs beneath tamarisks.

⑨ Visiting the sun-god

This trek to the chapel of the Prophet Elías takes eight to nine hours. The rural lanes at the beginning of the tour have lost their shade-providing trees following a forest fire. Later, for two hours, you wander all on your own along a rock path, which does however call for certain pathfinding skills and surefootedness too.

Those who are really afraid of heights may have difficulty at one point – but there are no truly exposed places. Several springs are to be found along the way. The tour should only be commenced in stable weather conditions – with food, sun and wind protection in the rucksack.

■ *18 km, difference in altitude 1,100 m, difficult*

▷ *Map see previous page*

AWT   Having arrived at the lower **car park** in **Marathókampos**
0.00   near the large church by taxi or the morning bus, you follow the sign "Pythagoras Cave" pointing uphill there. At
0.05   the end of the **cemetery** (left) you go right along a concrete track, up through a little pine forest. The track soon joins a rural lane, which winds its way uphill almost without any shade and comes to a transverse path. Here you go left along the almost level roadway through what remains of the forest fire of 2010.

On a hilltop (**P1:** N 37°43.599'/E 26°40.674', 395m) you turn off to the right and steeply uphill. At the top the path leads into a dip and, there, across a right turn-off of a

path. At the wayside shrine (right) you climb again, with
0.45 a fabulous view, up towards wind wheels. At the **roadway**
(**P2:** N 37°43.910'/E 26°40.894', 515m) you turn left at an
acute angle. Now comes a fairly long level stretch.

After the forest fire area the landscape becomes more
1.05 charming; to the left of the route stands a small **chapel**
and after another climb you can certainly do with the
well beside a cistern. Giant plane-trees line the roadway's
last ascent 1. Having passed a right turn-off, you reach,
1.40 on raised ground, the **monument** to the communist
fighters in the 1947/48 civil war who found hideouts in
the woods that existed at that time. They probably had
less time for the thrilling sea view.

Passing the wayside altar near the rock (left), you go
downhill for a bit – into the next burnt area. After 30 m
!! you therefore leave the roadway and climb *left up* on to a
path. Walking through isolated burnt trees, you arrive at a
green spot in the rocky landscape. Before the next valley,
likewise burnt, you saunter left through ferns which have
grown again in the meantime. Last tree remnants 2 line
the path leading to a small dip overlooking the sea (**P3:** N
37°44.165'/E 26°39.299', 775m).

2.00 After the burnt area orientation through the **rocky land-**
★ **scape** becomes more difficult, but at least the crosses
painted blue for the pilgrims are an aid. Now turning your
back on the sea, you climb again up to the right, along the
uppermost rocky outcrop (left). (The arrow on the yellow
sign points in the wrong direction!)

2.25 Passing through stunted trees, you head towards a **slop-**
ing ledge (**P4:** N 37°43.802'/E 26°38.899', 945m). Again
the blue crosses help you: first up right, then slightly

✓	downhill along a *hillside path,* which may cause nausea for the extremely sensitive hiker.
2.30	Quickly reaching a green **gully,** you ascend again up through open ground on the opposite side ③. After a rocky hilltop with sea view you traverse a "high macchia" strip (**P5:** N 37°43.558'/E 26°38'.427', 1080 m). Beyond it
2.55	a yellow **sign** points left, encouraging you with "500 m" – unfortunately it is a good deal further!
	Thereafter you proceed through "low macchia" and past a spring (sign). The next spring offers a shady, picture-book resting place. From there a short ascent leads up to the
3.15	**Chapel of the Prophet Elías (P6:** N37°43.148'/E26° 37.928', 1.100 m)

> *Countless peaks on the Greek islands are dedicated to the Prophet Elias, the Christian successor to the ancient sun-god Helios.*
>
> *In the chapel are two unusual panels depicting the prophet on a chariot of fire. Sadly the chapel is very dilapidated, but the view more than makes up for this.*

	From the chapel a path runs down across rock ledges towards the harbour on the horizon. Shortly afterwards the
!!	path turns off *to the right* and traverses a strip of macchia. Lined by stone pyramids, it reaches, after unpleasant
3.45	scree, a low **forest.**
4.05	Without any difficulty you reach the **Evangelístra Convent** ④ (**P7:** N 37°42.891'/E 26°38.427', 675 m), deserted and closed since 2009. However the well on the terrace is accessible. It is then an easy matter to go down the steps, right to the shady forest path and on to the upper end of
4.30	the **roadway** (**P8:** N 37°42.660'/E 26°38.424', 420 m).
	At first the descending roadway is a little bumpy, go left at the concreted fork further down. From there you drop down into the valley very pleasantly through olive
5.10	groves. At the **left turn** to the "Cave" you naturally go straight ahead and, with your last ounce of strength,
5.35	reach **Votsalákia beach.**

⑩ The Peak of Mount Kérkis

This nine to ten-hour walk in the mountains to the peak of Mount Kérkis leads through very different vegetation zones: olive groves, pine forests, mountain meadows, cliffs and rocks. You need to be in good physical condition, but vertigo is no problem. If you want to climb right up to the peak, you should start out no later than 7:00 am. Good weather is a necessity since sudden fog could make orientation very difficult, even though the entire stretch is marked. Your equipment should include sun lotion, protection against the wind and provisions. Water can be drawn at two places.
As a short cut, you could take a taxi to AWT 1.00.
■ *19 km, difference in altitude 1,440 m, difficult*

AWT	At the western edge of **Votsalákia** is the highly recommended restaurant "Anna" on the right side of the street.
0.00	Shortly after the **bridge** which follows is a sign "Cave of Pythagoras" pointing to the right. Follow the slightly ascending street, keeping to the left. After almost half an
0.25	hour comes a **fork** in the concrete road, where the track to the right leads to the cave ⑧, but you should bear left towards "Evangelístra".

The dirt road ascends slowly but steadily. Red arrows indicate the correct way through the olive groves, fresh in the morning dew. After the second rather long concrete stretch you go up steeply to the right at the right-angled fork. (It would be possible to drive this far with a taxi.) Af-

1.05	ter an ascent of 300 m you reach a small **turning area**

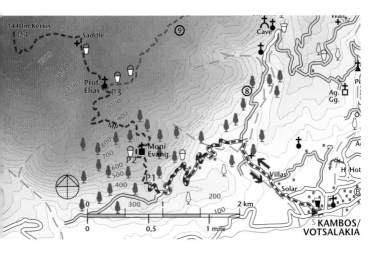

(**P1:** N37°42.660'/E26°38.424', 420 m).

A narrow path turns left up into the bushes. Well-marked with red diamond-shaped signs and dots, it winds through sparse pine woods ① and offers broad views across the sea where the fragmented islands of Foúrni are located. Soon the former **nunnery** ② (**P2:** N37°42.891'/E26°38.427') will shine from above on the left.

1.30

> *Moní Evangelístra, situated in pine woods at an altitude of 650 m, is only 60 years old. Although uninhabited since 2009, it does offer a well at the entrance.*

From the fence above the nunnery you wander up to the left into the lovely pine forest behind which the cliff face will later arise almost threateningly. With the scree above

2.00

the **edge of the forest** the more strenuous part of the trek begins. Then you have to cross through thorny kermes bushes and small mountain meadows ③ with a ***** view and the loveliest picnic spots of the day.

2.50

After a wide curve to the left you arrive at the **chapel to Profítis Elías** (**P3:** N37°43.148'/E26°37.928', 1100 m). Inside two panels depict the Prophet Elias hurtling through the sky on a sun chariot. He is the Christian descendant of the ancient sun god Helios. Firewood and blankets are kept in supply here for mountain emergencies. Otherwise you would hardly want to enter the dilapidated chapel.

At the tree above the chapel the path continues, first

through a mountain meadow and then along the left side of the mountain. On the right you can replenish your wa-
3.00 ter supply at a bubbling **spring.** Next you come to a small group of trees before the final ascent begins.
3.05 Behind the group of trees is a **mountain ridge** with a wayside shrine (left).

★ Already from here you have a wonderful view of the north side of Sámos, of Chíos and over into Turkey. You could turn back here – from now on it is only rubble and rocks. A challenge for real mountain goats.

The path continues on the right side of a mountain top ④, then leads across a ridge and, in a wide curve to the right, up to the peak of the Kérkis Mountains, in Greek
3.40 the "Vigla" (**P4:** N37°43.405′/E26°27.232′). This refers to an extinct volcano with a height of 1443 m asl. On clear days you can see very far: to the west as far as Ikaría, to the south Foúrni, Pátmos, Lipsí and Agathoníssi. Chíos and Lésbos are located to the north, and the continent of Asia is to the east.
4.20 You return the same way you came, to the **Profítis Elías chapel.** In the direction of the docks in Órmos Marathókampos you will find the continuation path which however swings to the right a little further on. It leads back to
5.10 the **nunnery** and, below it, on down to the **turning area.**
5.35 From there drag yourself thirstily down along the dirt ro-
6.00 ad and street to **Votsalákia.**

Diagonally across from the crossroads the shady garden taverna *"Vangélis"* awaits you with drinks, mesédes and beach chairs. You have really earned such self-indulgence today.

⑪ Three beaches…

… we will take in today: nobody knows the first one, a few the second and many the third. The four to five-hour hike runs almost entirely along roadways. First we traverse a ridge and enjoy the magnificent panorama of the south-west coast. Although it is difficult to find much shade, there are all the more springs and inns.
Start by taking a taxi to Kyriakí. The round trip via Limniónas is recommended with a hire car.
■ *11 km, diff. in altitude 250 m, easy to moderate*

AWT	
0.00	From the **car park** in **Kyriakí** (135 m) we proceed uphill and, 30 m beyond the well (left), left at the pink arrow. A concrete track runs alongside the stream-bed (left) below the village. In the shallow dip we take the road going left
0.05	and pass a **garage** beside four holiday houses (left). 10 m before the end of the road, on the right, appear more pink
0.10	arrows pointing to the **footpath** leading uphill (**P1**: N37°41.745'/E26°36.951'). This ends at ruts, which we follow to the left, later climbing. The ruts wind their way
0.25	up to the **hilltop** (250 m) ① (**P2**: N 37°41.536'/E 26° 36.994'). The sea!
0.30	We rush towards the water along roadways – but go uphill, right at the **fork**, for three minutes. The outstanding view stays with us along the way as we head towards the Foúrni islands ②. After a sharp left-hand bend we come
0.55	down to a **crossing**, where we go sharp right. Proceed along a narrow rural lane, past a left turn-off. From the end of the roadway a path drops down to the lonely little

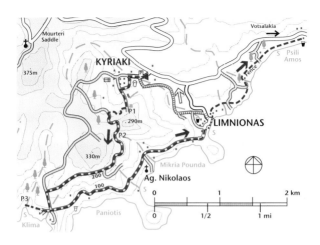

★   **beach** in **Klíma Bay** ③ ④ (**P3**: N37°40.478′/E26°36.056′).
1.05   (The first bit of the path continuing to Ioánnou Eleí-
        monas monastery is overgrown.)
        Between enormous boulders it is possible to stretch out
        and enjoy the sun and sea all on one's own; a cave can be
        reached by swimming. In the nearby stream fresh water
        gurgles until early summer – a small paradise for hikers...
        One has to drive oneself away from here and commence
        the walk back on the same path. Before Paniótis Bay we
1.20   **cross** the lane again and, further down, reach the "End of
        the world", a taverna which offers refreshments from
        June on.
        The panorama trail continues high above the sea as far as
1.35   **Míkria Poúnda Bay** ⑤. Vehicles are few and far between,

much to the chagrin of the owner of the "End of the world" of course. The grey Kérkis massif rises up above the charming bay, which we walk round before arriving at the

2.00 long beach of picturesque **Limniónas.** (From here a roadway leads to Kyriakí in 20 minutes, in case the hire car is waiting there.)

After shuffling along the beach, we encounter a footpath behind two building blocks. This first leads through a dry

2.10 stream-bed and then crosses a **gravel path.** The path runs through bushes directly above the cliff-lined coast until where a roadway takes us down into a dry stream-bed. Im-

2.20 mediately behind the **house in the dip** a path leads uphill, alongside a wire fence (right) and through a wonderful pine forest  and olive groves until joining a roadway.

!! Directly *in front of the house* standing there we continue,

2.35 later through branches, to **Psilí Ámos beach**, or "Fine sand". True! That is the reason our third beach and its inns are quite well frequented.

It is another three kilometres to Votsalákia.

⑫ Mondays only …

… is there a bus at 14.45 hours (please check!) from Drakëi to Karlóvassi – without it one has to plod back the whole way. The five-hour tour is one of the most beautiful in the Aegean – and almost entirely on shady trails. The spectacular Megálo-Seitáni Bay offers a long sandy beach, a few holiday houses being the only addition to the heavenly devil's bay. No wells or tavernas until Drakëi.

■ *11 km, difference in altitude 360 m, moderate*

AWT 0.00	It is best to take a taxi from Karlóvassi to the starting point at the **end of Potámia strand**, where concrete serpentine bends lead you uphill and past the left turn-off to Tsourléï. The roadway later begins a longer ascent at the "Dead End" sign, but you only follow it for a short bit.
0.15	Because your **path** begins after 200 m on the right – above a roadway. You quickly disappear in the olive groves, passing a wayside altar (left) as you do so. You are captivated by splendid views over to the Kérkis massif ①, before descending alongside gnarled olive trees to the wooden ramp at **Mikró-Seitáni Bay** ②.
0.40	
1.05	Having left the "Little Devil" behind you, you follow the undulating shady path ③ until you reach the **turn-off** to Kosmadéi ⑬. It is not necessary to undertake the arduous and difficult ascent, skipping down to the "Great Devil" instead. **Megálo Seitáni** – a strange name for this heavenly bay. (Or is there perhaps a snake lurking in the bushes?)
1.15	
★	The wide sandy bay is bordered by gigantic rock formations, which seem to reach up into the sky.

If you want to catch the bus in Drakëi, you should push on just before 13.00 hours – the alternative is to stay lazily stretched out and walk back.

Otherwise you can shuffle along the 400 m long strand

!! and, at the landing stage, already *before the two beach houses,* find the path half-left leading up the hill. Standing on the right behind the holiday houses is a wayside altar. Already before the path runs down into a veritable

1.30 jungle ravine, you pass **caves** (left). Then comes a more even stretch with nice views ④, before you go steeply uphill. At the next level stretch you discover a number of "oriental strawberry trees" with red trunks (p. 11).

2.10 Finally you turn your **back on the sea** (**P1:** N 37°45.857'/ E 26°36.955', 265 m) and wander up through an almost

2.20 healed forest fire area as far as the **wind gap,** the tour's highest point (**P2:** N 37°45.694'/E 26°37°.017', 360 m). Now you go downhill on an excessively wide roadway. (The plan was to continue this dirt road all the way to Megálo Seitáni, but thank goodness the money ran out.) In the valley bottom you ignore the two left turns, instead

2.40 taking a roadway up left immediately after the slight ascent. After 100 m you take the path to **Drakëi**, past an ikonísmo.

A pretty mountain village – where they build boats. And serve food and drink, if time still permits. But after this marvellous trek one is floating between heaven and earth and could survive on air alone.

Translation of special words for hikers

English	Français	Italiano	Nederlands	Svenska
boulder	bloc de rocher	masso	rotsblok	klippblock
cairn	marquage	segnalato di pietre	markeringssteen	vägmärke
cleft, ditch, dip	fossé	fosso	sloot	sänka
crest, ridge	crête	cresta	bergkam	bergskam
culvert	passage d'eau	passagio	waterleiding	vattenledning
defile	chemin creux	strada incassata	holle weg	hålväg
ford	gué	guado	wad	vadställe
fork, turn off	bifurcation	bifurcazione	wegsplitsing	vägskäl
gap	brèche	breccia	bres	inskärning
glade, clearing	clairière	radura	open plek in bos	glänta
gorge, ravine	gorge, ravine	abisso	kloof, Ravijn	ravin
gravel	pierraille	ghiaia	steengruis	stenskärvor
grove	bosquet	bosco	bosschage	lund
gully, incision	cours d'eau	letto di fiume	greppel	vattendrag
heath	bruyère	brughiera	heide	hed
hollow	dépression	depressione	glooiing	sänka
incline	pente	pendio	helling	sluttning
past	près de	accanto a	naast	jämte
pebble	caillou	ciottolo	kiezel	grus
pen	bergerie	stalla ovile	stal	stall
rift	fossée	fosso	sloot	sänka
rim	bords	orlo	rand	kant
rubble, scree	éboulis	ditriti	steengruis	stenar
saddle	crête	sella	bergrug	bergsrygg
schist	schiste	scisto	leisteen	skiffer
scrub	fourré	sterpaglia	doornbos	snår
slope	pente	pendio	helling	sluttning
stream bed	lit	letto di fiume	stroom bedding	vattendrag
strenuous	fatigant	faticoso	inspannend	ansträngande
well	puits	pozzo	bron	brunn

German version ISBN 978-3-9814047-2-2/Dutch version ISBN 978-3-9814047-4-6

⑬ Down to Satan's Bays

The Bays of Megálo and Míkro Seitáni, the "great and small Satans", can still only be reached on foot or by boat. Which makes this walk along the coast especially charming. As in ⑫, it is possible to get to know both bays by walking on this six-hour hike. At first it leads into the mountains above Karlóvassi and then ends up at the loveliest, flatter section of the famous coastal walk.

One should find out if the boat connection between Megálo Seitáni and Karlóvassi has been reinstated.

■ *18 km, difference in altitude 460 m, difficult*

AWT
0.00

In **Potámi** you follow the signs to the "Waterfalls" and reach the ancient church **Metamórfosis Sotiros** (s. p. 66) after three minutes. On the rock above it stands a Genoese castle ruin, the "Kástro".

Then you enter the tropically green ravine ☐ until, after eight minutes, the way on is blocked by a pond. (On the left a wildly-creatively nailed together wooden staircase leads up to the funny inn *Archodissa* and on to the waterfalls.) We however climb steeply up a path through the rocks opposite on the right.

0.15

Having arrived at the **top**, you see the frontal walls of the "Kástro" above the tree tops. From here a level path leads

0.20

to a wide **roadway** (**P1**: N37°46.957'/ E26°40.189', 130 m) and you turn left into it. Soon surfaced with concrete, it crosses over a hilltop (with right turn-off) and runs straight ahead through groves past a (hopefully still clo-

0.30

sed) garden tavern to the **church** in **Tsourléi** (left). *60 m*

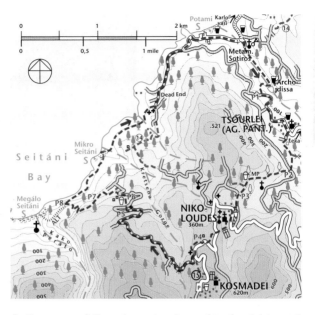

!!   *further on* you follow the water channel to the right, until this disappears in the bushes on the left *after 100 m.* Curious to discover where it goes, you find a jungle path on the right beside a grey reservoir. Alongside what is now a concreted channel this path leads you up to a transversal

0.45   **forest road** (**P2**: N37°46.403'/E26°40.482').

Cross over this and continue on a sunken path into a forest fire area (2001), which may make some slight detours necessary. A lovely kalderími ② will later lead through the slowly recovering landscape. When you walk under the trees once again, you will discover a spring (right) and a turn-off to the right which, however, you should disregard. Walk

1.05   *straight* on uphill and pass between two **houses** (**P3**: N37°46.227'/E26°39.914') at the top. The path then leads down into a fertile little valley with vineyards and olive trees. At the top you see houses and reach them quickly. There

1.10   is fresh water near the gigantic plane-tree in **Nikoloúdes** – a blessing after ascending the first 360 metres in altitude.

Stroll 120 m down the village street to the closed inn "Das goldene Herz" (left) and take the ramp immediately opposite up to the church. Beside the bell you go left and, 50 m

1.20	before the cemetery, right up a forest path to the **road** (chapel 50 m to your right). Immediately opposite a forest path takes you further, until it comes to the road again, which you take for 100 m to the right. After the guard rails,
!!	and before the left-hand bend, *steps lead right* back up into the forest (**P4:** N37°45.980/E26°39.688'). Again you come
1.25	to the **road** and have reached an altitude of 460 metres. Follow the sign "Μεγάλο Σεϊτavi" to the right and wander on a field track through vineyards in a wide curve to the right above a valley. Pass over a ford and later a bridge,
1.35	and then walk by two old **houses** (left). The wide sea is on the right as you slowly make your way downhill. Disre-
1.45	gard the horizontal turn-off to the left in a sharp **bend to the right** as well as a turn-off to the right in the following
1.55	curve to the left. You are only interested in a **red arrow** (**P5:** N37°46.201/E26°38.996') to the right of the concrete
!!	road which will lead you *to the right* on to an old mule track. It is somewhat overgrown, but can be followed. In case of doubt, keep to the right. Cross over the dirt road
2.00	again beside a **wayside altar** and continue on through thick bushes until you meet up with the concrete road again (**P6:** N37°46.303'/ E26°39.002') and go down it. A
2.05	shady **water basin** (left) appears at just the right time.
!!	20 m after two houses ③ pay attention: your rocky *path turns off* to the left in a right curve of the dirt road! Short-ly afterwards you will discover a terrace with olive trees
!!	and then walk *to the left* along the narrow path (not the wider path to the right!). At another terrace there are ve-
2.10	hicle tracks on the right – here, too, continue **downhill to the left** (**P7:** N37°46.330'/E26°38.818')! The way gets
★	nicer and nicer: sea, olive tree terraces, rockrose bushes ④.

Then follows quite a long flat stretch and another descent. Near the sea, *before a large grove of olive trees* and above the sandy bay, **the path forks.** A wooden sign marks the spot (**P8:** N37°46.257'/E26°38.430').

!!
2.25

Alternative: To arrive at the broad, sandy bay of **Megálo Seitáni,** walk ten minutes *to the left* (p. 76).

If you would like to wander back, however, walk to the right along the **turn-off** mentioned above and meander through thick greenery, enchanted by the chirping of birds. A wooden ramp leads to the beach at **Míkro Seitáni** (p. 58). From there, ramble through rocks, meadows and terraces of olive trees past a field shrine to the **dirt road** and follow it downhill to the left.

2.25
2.45
3.05

Walk straight on, disregarding any turn-offs, until you arrive at the beach in **Potámi.** You could take a look at the ancient *church of Metamórfosis Sotiros,* dating partially from the 6th century.

3.20

It is recommendable to look for a bus or some other vehicle in Potámi since it takes another 25 long minutes on asphalt along the street to return to the harbour in Karlóvassi.

⑭ Along mule tracks

... is where this marvellous six-hour hike leads us through olive groves to a wide sandy beach, to cave churches and to a pretty village square. To shorten it, take a taxi to Potámi, or catch one back from Léka. Along the way are inns and places with water. In addition to your water bottle, an electric torch is useful.

■ *17 km, diff. in altitude 390 m, moderate to difficult*

AWT 0.10   Follow walk 15 from **Karlóvassi-Limáni (harbour)** to the inn "**Grados**". A ramp on the right of the parking area leads uphill (seaward) along Galáta street to the church (right). After three minutes is a chapel ☐ on the right with a playground, where you walk straight on. Stone slabs which have been walked on for centuries lead past the

0.15   Cosmas and Damian **chapel in a grotto** and on up to a clearing at the top of the path, to the right of which is a wayside shrine (**P1**: N37°47.538'/E26°40.680', 160m).

0.20   To the left of the shrine a path leads down to the **Saint Antónios cave church.** If you haven't brought along an electric torch, take some candles inside with you in order to experience the magic of the high prayer room in the back section.

Once you are outside and on the way uphill again, the path leads through a tunnel of kermes oaks until you notice a

0.25   **turn-off** to the right leading down to the Paraskeví Chapel. Beneath the branches of a cracked plane-tree is a marvellous rest area with a spring framed by terraces of olive trees. Back up on the main path again, walk down to the right,

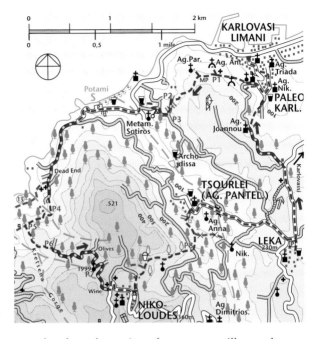

past the charred remains of trees; you will soon have a view of the modern chapel at the beach in Potámi and come to a **dirt road** (**P2**: N37°47.405'/E26°40.346'). (A holiday home is located in the rocks on the right). Wander on to the left, disregarding two turn-offs, and then later turn off to the right on to a concrete street leading downhill (**P3**: N37°47.391'/ E26°40.187'). The street has a curve to the right after about 200 m and here you should turn off to the left on to a **forest path.** A small wall accompanies you on the right. One minute later – after a curve to the left and *directly before a clearing* – turn off sharply to the right on to a footpath leading to the **street** in **Potámi.**

0.35

0.40

!!

0.45

> *On the right there are two very nice inns.*
> *On the left, 60 m further, friends of art, nature and picnics can enjoy an excursion to the oldest church on the island, Panagía Toú Potamíou (or Metamórfis) ②, 4 min. away. The unusually tall church was constructed in the 11th century. The four marble pillars are probably 500 years older than that and originate from the monastery*

which existed then. Some ruins of a Genoese castle keep watch on a rock overlooking it.

0.55 The street leads to a **parking area** at the end of the beach, and, from there, a concrete path brings you uphill. The

1.00 **turn-off** to the left towards Léka is of no interest. Instead, look up to Mount Kérkis, the highest mountain on Sámos

1.10 ⑩. Continue uphill, even when you reach the **turn-off** to the right ("Dead End"). After 200 m the dirt road and path on the right lead off to Seitáni Bay. Disregard them and walk straight on uphill, past a field altar (right) and a

1.15 turn-off to the left, until you come to where the **dirt road ends** above a fork (**P4:** N37°46.811'/E26°39.276').

The hiker's territory begins two metres to the left of an old olive tree ③: Having touched the dirt road again, you see a house on the right on the opposite slope about 60 metres

1.20 away, cross a small **furrow** and the go *immediately left* up

!! through the undergrowth of a pine forest. After six minutes – back in the open again – you have to watch out: Af-

1.25 ter 20 m ④ a **meadow path** turns off *up to the left* at right

!! angles (**P5:** N37°46.623'/E26°39.038'). (If you went on another 50 m, you would see the Megálo Seitáni).

Our path climbing to the left is sufficiently well marked,

1.35 but further up it comes to a new, rough **roadway** (**P6:** N37°46.562'/E26°39.090', 195 m).

We go along it to the right and straight ahead. After a

1.50 quarter of an hour you ignore both the **right turn-off** in the forest and, five minutes later, the left turn-off into an olive grove. We are not satisfied until we have reached the

2.00 **Chapel of 1999** (**P7:** N37°46.381'/E26°39.682', 200 m).

At the next fork after 80 m, bear right and walk past vine-

2.10 yards (right, with cottage) until you arrive at the **street.**

2.15 Walk along it to the left and then downhill in curves until you come to the gigantic plane-tree in **Nikoloúdes**, where you can treat yourself to delightful spring water.

Hop down three steps next to the plane-tree, take the path leading downhill, then the lane going left through the olive groves. After a hollow, a path leads between two

!!
!! houses and, behind them immediately *to the right,* down through a pine forest. *Disregard* the flagstone path which leads up to the left shortly afterwards and, instead, keep walking downhill, where you will soon cross through a forest fire area which is becoming green once again ⑤.

2.35 Later cross a **forest road** (**P8:** N37°46.403'/E26°40.482'); the trail descends further, accompanied by a square-shaped open water channel (right). After five minutes you disregard the overgrown path (right), but at the bottom

2.45 take the lane going right, to **Tsourléi.** (The village alley would take you left back Potámi in 20 minutes.)

Walking to the right along the street, across a stream bridge and uphill, you arrive at the lovely **square in Léka**,

3.20 with its tavernas and a magnificent view across the coun-

★ tryside. Let yourself be pitied by the innkeeper Nikos first of all, and then have him bring you something to drink.

The rest can be told briefly: refreshed, walk out of the village along the same way you came. At the parking area, continue straight on, slightly uphill at first over a hilltop.

3.35 After 200 m, at the **sign** "Moni Ioannou", turn to the left, where you have a majestic view of the sea ⑥. Before the

3.45 **Monastery to Saint John,** turn off to the right on to a footpath which leads downhill. At a yellow house on the

3.55 right, walk left down the steps to the taverna "Grados"

4.05 again, where you turn right and walk down to **Karlóvassi.**

⑮ Away up in Kosmadéi

This varied, six to seven-hour hike follows rural lanes and paths up through farming and wooded countryside to the highest village on Sámos. There, and in two further villages, the hiker can expect to find tavernas or at least springs.

Returning by taxi as far as Léka or from Nikoloúdes makes the trip much easier. Those with a hire car start in Léka.

■ *17 km, difference in altitude 620 m, difficult*

AWT	
0.00	In **Karlóvassi-Limáni** you go uphill from the main street at the sign "Paleo". Then, four minutes later, left across
0.08	the bridge and up the old paved pathway to a **square.** Here you go right, right again at the next fork, come past the three-nave St. Nicholas' church (left) and arrive at the
0.10	taverna "**Grados**".
	Beside it on the right you take the steps up to Aggelinidi alley, which you walk along for a while before disappearing into a wood. In front of a yellow house you take the
0.20	stone path up right to the **Ágios Ioánnou Convent.** From there a roadway overlooking the sea leads you on to the main street, where you march right to Léka.
0.50	From the wide **platía**, where idleness was invented a long long time ago, you take the steps leading uphill to the right of the *períptero*, a "small department store". The alley ends at a tiny square (gap site), where you go right. After a left-hand bend you go up right at the T-junction. (The village church on the right cannot be seen). On the left is a valley with gardens.

At the end of the village you cross a **street** ①; on the left stands an *ikónisma*, a wayside shrine (**P1**: N 37° 46.266'/E 26°41.166', 230 m). A rural lane then leads you along the edge of the wood and over a hilltop. Soon the next destination comes into view: Kastaniá ②. At a sizeable **fork** (left a high retaining wall) you continue climbing on the narrower lane straight ahead, until you reach a **road** (**P2**: N 37°45.847'/E 26° 41.002). On it you descend right, past a chapel (right), into a wooded valley as far as a **bridge.**

0.55

1.05

1.10

1.15

Immediately behind this you turn left on to a forest path which runs above a stream. It ends after five min-

!! utes. (On the right are pump stations and, concealed, a chapel). Proceed another *ten metres straight ahead* and then turn left into a dry bed. There, after another ten metres, you find stones heaped up on the left and, above them, the entrance to a forest path. This takes you up to an olive grove in three minutes and, to the right of same, on uphill.

1.25 Above the grove you encounter a **rural lane** leading right. At the junction after 50 m (**P3**: N 37°45.495'/E 26°40.934') you take the wider roadway left. After another minute, at the fork beside a shed (right), you saunter right up through more olive groves until the lane ends up on a terrace.

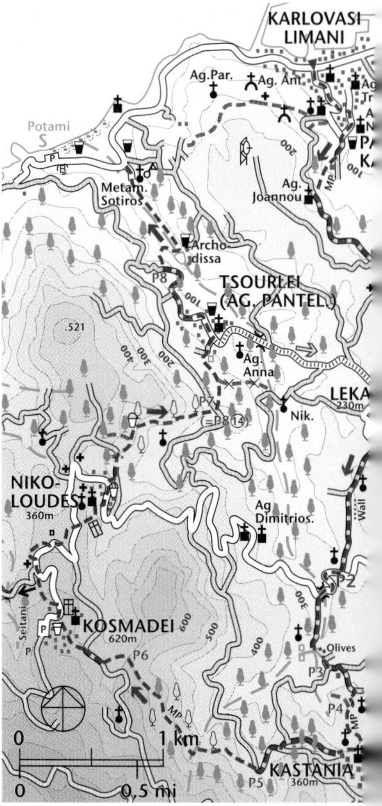

Following footprints, you stalk up through the retaining walls and discover – a monopáti. That just had to come! (**P4:** N 37°45.367'/ E 26°41.039'). Where it forks at an acute angle, you go left and later, past the right-hand vineyard chapel ③, up into the beautiful and unspoilt village of **Kastaniá.**

1.35

On the left, a little lower down, stands the memorial to the village inhabitants who were shot by Italian occupation forces in 1943 in retaliation for partisan attacks.

Below the church head left for the platía with taverna and chestnut tree. From there you go back again and, proceeding below the church, past a chapel (right) to the **end of the village**, which is accentuated by a hen-coop.

1.40

A forest path leads you uphill and forks after six minutes. Go up left and, after 40 metres, right. Ten metres beyond a sharp *right-hand bend in a trough* you must watch out:

!!

1.50

An old **forest path** leads uphill there! (**P5:** N 37°45.130'/E 26°40.607', 375 m). It winds its way up steeply towards a rocky face ④. The stock of trees was severely depleted by the fire in 2002. By way of compensation, though, you have the view over the broad valley and the Ámpelos mountains beyond.

When you later come on to a broad ridge (**P6:** N 37°45.493'/E 26°40.013', 555 m), stay below the roadway initially. Do not use it until you see the first houses up above. In a dipping right-hand bend you later leave it and go up left on to the paved pathway leading to **Kosmadéi.**

2.25

You have now reached the highest village on Sámos, 620m above sea level, which calls for a drink right here on the platía (which also serves as the car park).

The descent begins on the steps in front of the church.

2.35	Having taken the road at the bottom, you leave it ten me-tres beyond the cemetery, dropping left on to a short-cut path. It re-joins the road, where the **branch-off** to Megá-lo-Seitáni Bay soon follows on the left.
!!	Immediately to the *right of the concrete ramp* next to the wayside altar a concealed path runs downhill. Alas, after three minutes it once more ends at the road. Further down, however, at the road's next right-hand bend, you can soon disappear again left into the bushes and play ranger.
2.40	Having again reached the **road**, you find opposite it – slightly to the left – the continuation of the forest path. This leads downhill and ends at the church of
2.50	**Nikoloúdes**. Taking the steps down from there brings you straight to the *"Goldene Herz"*, a former taverna. Wa-ter can be drawn next to the giant plane-tree, further up to the left. From here you follow the description for walk
3.20	⑭ (p. 68) to **Tsourléi** (and, where appropriate, to Léka). On the narrow village street you go left (north) past church (right) and garden taverna. After about 10 min-utes you leave it, taking a path to the right (**P8:** N37°46.957'/ E26°40.189'), which brings you into the val-
3.45	ley and thence left to **Potámi.**

▷ Those interested in learning more about Sámos will find further background information in "The Greek Islands" by Paul Hetherington (London, 2001) and "Samos with Ikaria & Fourni" by Nigel McGilchrist (London, 2010).

⑯ A mystical spring

The destination of the four to five-hour hike is the romantic spring of Petaloúdas and the oldest and most beautiful frescoes on Sámos. The trail leading there also takes in the unspoilt village of Ydroússa. The tour, which offers plenty of shade, runs mostly on rural lanes – the last stretch on a side road. Ydroússa and Kondakeíka have places to stop for a bite to eat. Please check the bus timetable for the return journey!

■ *12 km, difference in altitude 330 m, moderate*

AWT From the **bus station** in **Karlóvassi** go uphill, in other
0.00 words with the car park and children's playground on the
left, keep left at the top and in this way walk round the
"Health Centre" (right) in a right-hand arc. Later you turn
up left at the rear corner of the cemetery near the cypresses. 50m after that you go right at an acute angle on a roadway and, on the edge of the pine forest, steeply upwards.
Having passed the large school (left), you come to a concrete path, which you follow up over a hilltop as far as a
0.10 **junction.**
The roadway heading left looks interesting – so take it. After 150m go straight ahead at the left turn-off to the St.
0.15 Catherine's Chapel and up to a **crossroads** (**P1**: N 37°
47.533'/E 26°42'.787', 115 m). To the left lies the valley of
Fourniótikos, above it the village of Kondakeíka, which
you will visit at the end of the tour.
At this crossroads you go left, past a villa and on through
pines and olive trees. The forest path runs downhill, past

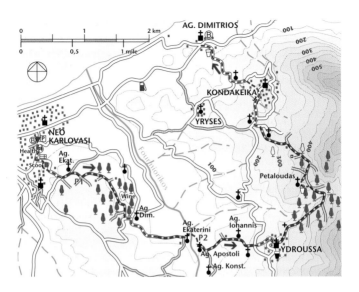

0.30   a concrete ramp (left) to a **clearing with vineyards** ①.
Back in the forest, you go left at the fork and come to the
road, where you descend left for 20 m and, already before

0.35   the **Dimítrios Chapel**, walk to the right.
The road, later a rural lane, passes through farming coun-
try with vines and olives as far as the chapel **Agía
Ekateríni** (1898). Immediately in front of this you turn

0.50   off left and, in a right-hand arc, arrive at the **stream** (P2:
N 37°46.939'/E 26°44'.064', 80 m).
Traverse it on stones, bear right further up before reaching
the meadow and, this time in a left-hand arc, proceed to
the chapel **Agíi Apóstoli.** From there a concrete path
leads up to a rural lane, which you take up to the left. It
climbs leisurely through vineyards, turns right at the fork

1.05   in front of a house and later runs past the **St. John's
Chapel.** Three minutes beyond it you reach a crossroads.
Continue straight ahead uphill, but immediately in front
of a house in a left-hand bend turn right on to a mono-

1.15   páti. After 30m this leads right to **Ydroússa.**
At the fork you go up left to the (lower) church, bordered
on either side by kafenía. Before trekking on you might
like to explore the twisted alleyways a little or have something to drink. From the church forecourt (with the

nailed-on letter box) you go up a narrow alley, turn off right and then come, to the right of the black garden fence, into the "Kapetan Alley". At the bench you leave the village again by going right on a nice concrete path,

1.20 which runs past a small **"ikonísma guardhouse"** (left), in a happy mood.

What becomes a forest path leads you up to a T-junction in 17 minutes (**P3:** N 37°47.190'/E 26°45°.441', 330 m). Here you go left down the concrete path to the little ford and up again on the other side of the stream. 120 m further on, after a right turn-off, comes a level stretch. Five

1.40 metres beyond where *the next climb begins* is a **path** on
!! the left (**P4:** N 37°47.261'/E 26°45°.384', 115 m).

★ Spread out 50 m further down is a quintessentially Greek, almost mythical idyll: the spring of **Petaloúdas** beneath four enormous plane-trees and a romantic festive site. The Assumption of Mary Chapel further down possesses exceptionally beautiful frescoes with magnificent faces, probably from the 13th century. Depicted are among others two rows of prophets with their writings ②.

From the spring you go back up to the forest lane (2ⁿᵈ turn-off!) and thence left, past a black water tank (left). Ascending slightly, you come to a broader roadway, where you go left down through a forest and olive groves.

1.55 Disregard the wide **left turn-off** to house ruins. Instead you go straight ahead through a forest fire zone (2001), then downhill and, on a level stretch, past a farmhouse
!! (left). Where *the fence ends* (before the climb), cairns then point left!

Going this direction, the roadway becomes a path after 50m and widens out again further down. It runs straight

2.05 on through a dip and, next to a **chapel** (right), comes to a concrete road. Success, you have done it!

Here you go down left and, at the intersection with the car park, down right towards the houses. If you have no more time for a break, go left at the edge of Kondakeíka village, shortly after the bridge. Before the pylons with power distributor you swing down left and, 50m further on, right. A level path leads you to steps and to a ramp,

2.20 which brings you to the **road.** Dash down it to **Áyios**
2.30 **Dimítrios** if you want to catch the bus at 17.00 hours.

⑰ In the Vineyards of Stavrinídes

Today's walk takes you to where the famous wine from Sámos is made. The excursion lasts four to five hours, of which one is spent on kalderímia! Magnificent views across the landscape with its green terraces and the blue sea are your reward. There are tavernas in the two mountain villages and several fountains along the way. At times you walk along paths which are hardly used any more and which might be partially overgrown. For this reason, long trousers and long-sleeved shirts are recommended in order to overcome the natural hindrances and avoid using the roads.

■ *9.5 km, difference in altitude 550 m, difficult*

AWT
0.00   The tour begins by wandering uphill at the wooden sign "Stavridídes" next to a fountain on the **main street** in **Ayios Konstantínos**. After a few metres you use an old kalderími until you arrive at a concrete street, where you continue on uphill to the left. In the grape vines on the
0.05   left is the **chapel to Constantine**, one of the symbols of Sámos ①. You can see the lovely wooden iconostasis through a window.

50 m further on, after the plane-tree and the fountain in the part of the village called **Ano Ayios Konstantínos**, you turn off right onto a welcoming lane, and at its end another lane leads on uphill to the left. You pass by a church on the left two minutes later and continue along a cobbled path and then uphill to the left at the next
0.08   **wooden sign** (**P1**: N37°48.285'/E26°48.824').

After four minutes you meet the dirt road for the first time. Red diamond-shaped symbols guide the hiker along the following stretch and lead to the left here. After 60 m, before a retaining wall, turn uphill to the right onto a narrow path. You arrive at the dirt road again, follow it to the left for 50 m and then ascend to the right, using a kalderími. Generations of farmers and their mules have tramped along its cobblestones. Later the path narrows, leads through groves and circles around a house (left). Then it

0.25 meets up with the **dirt road** for a third time.

Once again you continue uphill to the left, passing ruins with cypress trees (left), and then leave the dirt road after 80 m, beyond a curve to the right (**P2:** N37°47.995'/ E26°49.014'). You have the cobblestones to accompany you here until you reach the road once again. Continue walking uphill, again at the turn-off in a right-hand bend,

0.40 past a **cemetery** and into **Stavrinídes** (390 m).

At the telephone booth, take the lane going right to the

0.45 **church.** If you fancy something to eat, you can stop at "Irida" on the right. Walk up the steps beside the church and well ② and, at the top, turn left beside a well onto a steep concrete path. Hardly have you had time to work up a sweat than, after two minutes, the way becomes leisure-

0.50 ly. At the **sign** "Ay. Panteleimon", turn right up a mule track. Accompanied by water distributors, continue

1.05 climbing along the shady path ③ until you arrive at a **dirt road** in the vineyards at the top.

*At an altitude of 550 metres you are in the midst of the terraces where the famous golden coloured island wine **Samaína** grows best. Vineyards can be found up to an altitude of 900 metres. Wine has been cultivated on Sá-*

mos for 3,000 years, though in those days it was red and
rather astringent. Later it even reached the status of "al-
tar wine" in the Vatican. And Lord Byron wrote the im-
mortal lines:
"In vain – in vain: strike other chords;
Fill high the cup with Samian wine!
Leave battles to the Turkish hordes,
And shed the blood of Scio's vine!"
The grapes – mainly muscat grapes – are harvested in
September and processed in large press houses in Vathí
and Karlóvassi.

Withstand the enticement of the path leading on uphill
and instead meander to the right, beneath shady walnut
trees, along the slightly ascending and later descending

1.10 dirt road. Behind a glen you meet up with a wider **track**
(sign "Lakka"). Go down it to the right and, after bends,
past a wayside shrine (right). Then come red tin shacks

!! (right) and, 130 m further, an *indistinct crossing with a*
narrow path (**P3:** N37°47.822'/E26°48.089'). Here you
head right into the bushes and follow the path until it
meets a concrete track beside a prominent rock (right).

As the former path down to Ámpelos is overgrown from
here on, you unfortunately have to use the concrete track
round several bends until, beyond a quarry (left) where a

1.30 lane turns off to the left, you see a **telephone antenna**
(**P4:** N37°47,958'/E26°48,221'). You turn off towards it
and follow, with a view of the sea ④, the country and, lat-

1.35 er, concrete track. Below a **house** you turn off right and,

1.40 at the end, find a narrow paved path (p. 89) to **Ámpelos**
(290 m). The name of the village means "vineyard", but
the houses look rather sober.

Near the upper church are two inns. Nice steps at the rear
of the church lead down to a car park. Walk along to the
right with a magnificent view and then downhill to the

1.45 left at the fork in the street. 50 m beyond the covered **well**
(1991, right) take a sharp turn to the left and you will see
a water basin on the right after 30 m. At the end of the
wide path, follow a path to the right towards the sea, just
as the water hose does.

The path winds left, follows the contour lines and for
some time slightly descends the slope. After a vintner's
cottage (right) (**P5:** N37°48.229'/E26°48.069', 225 m) you
encounter a concrete track and, 200 m further down, a

1.55	**junction**, where you turn off right onto a lane. With the sun warming your back, it is a pleasure to stroll on
2.05	through the gardens to the **road.**
!!	Go up it for *50 m to the right,* where on the left you find *large stones* leading a few metres down to a kalderími. This runs right, down into the valley, where later, up in the woods, you can spot the optically distorted forest chapel to Saint Nicholas.
	Further downhill you turn left at a wide dirt track through the woods and turn off to the right after 100 m, passing
2.15	the valley floor and coming back to the **church** of **Áno Áyios Konstantínos.** At the fountain and the plane-tree, saunter downhill along the street. 150 m below the much-photographed white chapel, a kalderími leading to the
2.25	right brings you back to **Áyios Konstantínos** and the main street.

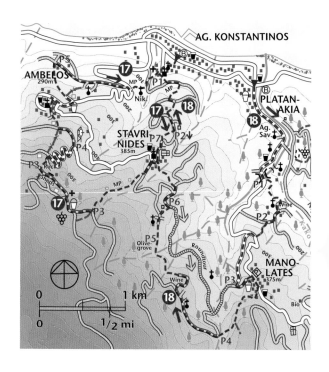

⑱ Panorama

The region around Áyios Konstantínos is considered to be the greenest on the island. In five to six hours you walk in a great circle along old paths on mountain ridges and pass through two old villages.
You should be able to orientate yourself well in thick bushes and have a certain amount of physical fitness. There are springs along the way.
The trail can easily be reached by bus. Those with a hire car can take a circular walk around Manolátes.
■ *11 km, difference in altitude 390 m, moderate*

▷ *Map see previous page*

AWT	In **Platanákia**, east of Áyios Konstantínos, walk inland
0.00	along the street towards Manolátes. In the Nightingale Val-
0.10	ley continue past the small chapel of **Áyios Sávas** (right)
0.18	and later some excursion inns until you come to a **bridge**

beyond which, after 10 m on the left beside a water channel, our footpath begins ① (**P1:** N37°47.649'/E26°49.696'). It changes into a wonderful paved way leading uphill.
Bear right at the next fork of the path and right again at the dirt road further up. Then walk uphill through vine-

0.25 yards to the left of a **chapel** and thereafter ascend to the right beneath a house. Turn to the right onto a flat dirt road at the next junction and enjoy the pleasant vineyard landscape as you proceed. But pay attention! 20 m be-

!! yond the fork, at some *cairns* above the group of houses
0.30 in the vineyard, a **footpath** turns off uphill to the left ② (**P2:** N37°47.423'/E26°49.607', 160 m).

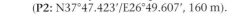

★   You wander in reverie along delightful steps past sparse terraces of olive trees ③ and enjoy a view of the Turkish coast until guard rails remind you that you are in the 21st

0.35 century. Striding downhill along the **street** you reach, after 80 m, a ramp which leads up left to the strenuously steep concrete road in the direction of Ountades. At the

0.50 very top, at the **fork** (P3: N37°47.047'/E26°49.443') you

0.55 turn left to **Manolátes** (375 m).

As you wander around the lovely village, you notice a lot of houses decorated with flowers and several potters' workshops. At the taverna "Despina" near the square with the covered well, walk uphill for 20 m, then turn to the right twice. To the right of seven steps you discover a path in which there are also water lines. Stavrinídes can be seen on the right of the slope on the opposite side.

1.00 Walking to the left at the **water basin** which follows, you discover a solitary path ④ leading through the lovely hilly

1.05 countryside. At a **fork** with a pine tree, bear right and

1.10 head steeply downhill into the **stream bed** (P4: N37° 46.909'/E26°49.363', 320 m).

Follow the dirt road there uphill to the left and, at the chapel ⑤, you might decide to have a rest with a lovely

1.20 view of Manolátes ⑥. At the **fork** (sign) 300 m further on, continue downhill to the right and then turn to the left at a sharp angle around a vineyard further down. In the woods which follow, glide as elegantly as Apache Indians

★   through two wooded valleys with olive trees between

1.35 them. Afterwards, walk uphill into an **olive grove** (P5: N37°47,269'/E26°48,866'). At its *lower edge,* you can find markings leading to a dirt road and an inconspicuous

1.40 **chapel** with a house (left). 50 metres beyond the concrete crossing is a coarsely levelled dirt road leading downhill to the right. At its lower end, a somewhat overgrown

1.50 mule track leads further on downhill to a **dirt track** (**P6:** 37°47.499'/E26°49.036').

> *Round tour:* To the right this leads back to the stream bed (AWT 1.10) and the path leading up to **Manolátes.**

Otherwise, wander to the left for five minutes along this dirt road until you see a blue sign indicating a narrow
1.55 path 10 m beneath a wide **fork.** At the washhouse in the
2.00 valley walk up the steps to arrive at **Stavrinídes** (385 m). You can take a well-earned rest in the taverna "Irida" in the middle of the village.

At the church the next lovely footpath begins, leading
2.05 downhill first past a telephone box, then past the **ceme-tery** (right) and on under cypress trees and pines. Later
!! you come to a dirt road and after seven minutes see *cairns* in a curve to the right (**P7:** N37°48.021'/E26°48.971'). They indicate the old footpath to the left, which later meets up with the dirt road again. Follow the road to the
!! left until you see a house down on the right. *50 m before it the old footpath* leads further on downhill. After reaching the road again, you have another 50 m to the left until you come to the next short-cut, which turns off steeply downhill. Walk along the next piece of the road for one minute before walking down to the right.

The path becomes a wide kalderími leading to the old
2.35 church of **Áno Áyios Konstantínos.** Beneath the main church you arrive at a chapel (title photo). 150 m further down, another fine flagstone path to the right directs you
2.40 down to the main street which passes through **Áyios Konstantínos.**

⑲ The prettiest villages on Sámos

Two of the prettiest villages on the island, Vourliótes and Manolátes, are along the route of this fantastic, five to six-hour hike. Half of the tour follows shady paths, the first ascent a former kalderími. Both villages boast pleasant inns, springs are also to be found along the way.

■ *13 km, diff. in altitude 370 m, moderate to difficult*

AWT

0.00

Get the local bus to stop at the turn-off to **Kámbos-Vourliótes**, so that you can alight. Beside the south side of the street is a sort of **car park**, from where a concrete path, a former kalderími, leads uphill.

0.05

Below the group of houses in Paleochóri (left) lies the 14th century chapel **Ayía Pelágia**, whose interior is unadorned. 100 m further you come to the chapel **Ayía Matróna** on the right, which as well may be as old as 600 years ①. It, on the other hand, accommodates frescoes depicting Old Testament scenes from the 17th century.

0.10

0.15

Now you head for the wooded hills; after a large pool (right) the trail, accompanied by water channels, becomes quite steep. After 8 minutes the roadway branches left to Avlákia beyond a **house** (directly on the left, after a chapel) ㉓ (**P1:** N37°47.626'/E26°50.944', 140 m). Go straight ahead (on the old paving stones at last) and, at the fork, left to **Pnaká**. It is possible to drink the water from the springs, or consume other beverages in the shady taverna.

Proceed on up the concrete kalderími, after three minutes left at the fork and left again at a tall concrete retaining

wall. First on paving, then on concrete you reach the edge of the village and, at the war memorial, go up right to the

0.40 **platía of Vourliótes** (340 m). A wonderful place to rest in the midst of the winding alleyways, whose architecture is reminiscent of Asia Minor, where the founders of the village hailed from.

Leave the square at the letter box on a level alley, along which, after 80 m, you see a small well on the right. Five metres further you turn off right and, further down, left at the pylon of an electricity transformer. Walking alongside the cemetery (left), you come to an old defile. Where it

0.45 ends, you march left on a shady **roadway**, until this swings left uphill after three minutes ②. But you do not,

!! instead going slightly downhill on a *path straight ahead*. After 10 m the path forks (**P2:** N 37°47.253'/E 26°50.531').

!! (To the right it leads to Platanákia.) You continue *straight ahead* and immediately encounter a forest path which leads, later through olive groves, to the **chapel Àyios Spiridónas** ③.

Immediately on the right of the chapel a shady forest

1.05 path brings you in 15 minutes to the bed of the **Kakórema**, the "bad stream". On the other side, 10 m over to the left, a path runs past a waterfall to a roadway 100 m away.

!! Take this for *20 m to the right,* where markings indicate an ascending track.

> **Short cut:** The roadway leads along the stream in Nightingale Valley to Platanákia in 20 minutes.

The steeply ascending track gets flatter after ten minutes near terraced vineyards (right) ④ and becomes a roadway above the terraces. Where it forks, climb left uphill and later disregard a left turn-off. On a fairly long level stretch you can enjoy the view down into Nightingale Valley, before the roadway becomes a concrete road.

Go 100 m left along the road until you see a mule track on the right which later ends up on concrete again. Go right

1.40 there, past the cemetery (left), to **Manolátes** (380 m), a very pretty place, in which a fair bit of pottery is made. Order a glass in one of the cosy inns and drink to your achievement.

Below the taverna "Déspina" at the covered well stands the town hall with important public facilities: telephone box and letter box. And there on the left is also where your way out of the village commences, down a concrete

1.45 road and down right at a **fork** (**P3:** N37°47,047'/E26° 49,443'). The going is quite steep from here for a while, but partly in the shade, down the concrete road to the asphalt road and then 80 m up right to the bend.

At the end of the guardrails are steps on the left, which lead you down a wonderful paved track winding its way through olive groves. Where it finishes, follow the level

2.05 **roadway** to the right (**P4:** N37°47,423'/E26°49,607', 160 m), turn off left and, immediately below a house

!! (right), left again. At the chapel (left) you veer right – but

2.10 *only for 50 m!* **Left** is where you go, along terraced old vineyards (right), down to the

2.15 **road** in the valley.

You take the wooden bridge after 100m, climb up the steps, go right in front of the houses at the top, weave your way between two sheds in slalom style and look for the path down to the stream. On the far side of the stream a

2.25 shady narrow **forest path** leads, later across a concrete ford,

2.40 to **Platanákia**.

㉜ Water and Wine

... but also olives can be savoured on this short walk through Arcadian rural landscapes. And, as the climax, an idyllically situated taverna where one can enjoy other things as well. The two to three-hour tour on country lanes and paths can be done as a round trip too.

■ *6 km, difference in altitude 200 m, easy*

▷ *Map see previous page*

AWT
0.00

In the coastal plain of **Kámbos-Vourliótes** you leave the wide main road at the hamlet **Tsárli.** A concrete track leads into one of the best locations for Sámos wine, which used to be shipped here directly on the coast. The large old wine warehouse on the road to Platanákia still bears testimony to those days.

After three minutes you turn up left and soon ramble through a wonderful olive grove. On the left in the valley stands the 600-year old *Pelágia Chapel* ⬚; a little later you also see the *Matrónis Chapel* on a hill to the left, which likewise dates back to the 14th century. The trail then be-

0.15

comes more wooded, runs above a fairly large **dwelling** (right) and – without turning up to the left! – through a sylvan hollow and up to a fork (**P1:** N37°47.780′/E26° 50.423′, 75 m).

There you go up left on a concrete track and, at the electricity meter box of a holiday house, up to the right, as far as another **electric meter** on the right ⬚. Here you will find *markings on the left* into an old path which begins be-

0.20
!!

0.25 hind a holiday house. It leads up the course of a stream in the shade to a **country lane** (**P2:** N37°47.670'/E26° 50.554').

A truly "Greek" pastoral landscape greets the rambler, who should continue up to the right from here. After a few metres you go left at the fork, then past four holiday log cabins (left) and across more turn-offs. Further up you stay on the same level as far as a parapet wall (left) ③ at a turn-off to the right (**P3:** N37°47.537'/E26°50.842', 160 m).

Here you leave the lane by turning left, where you discover another monopáti through a green valley cutting. Where the path forks, you climb right and find, at the

0.40 **Pnaká springs** (200 m), one of the most idyllic garden tavernas on the Greek islands ④.

Having enjoyed that, you leaf on to page 100 to read the

1.15 description of how to get to **Tsaboú Strand.**

The description for a **circular tour** back into the Kámbos plain can also be consulted there. The two old chapels are on this route.

㉑ Vourliótes

... is not only the high point of the three to four-hour hike, which leads up through shady forests to the old town from the coastal village of Platanákia, on account of its altitude; the popular path from there leads down to Kokkári.

Hire car drivers may consider the combination with ⑲ as a round trip. No springs, but the nice tavernas in Vourliótes certainly make amends.

■ *10.5 km, difference in altitude 340 m, moderate*

AWT
0.00 From the **bus stop** next to the garden inn *Apolarsi* in **Platanákia** you march off into the valley of the nightingales on the road to Manolátes. At low water one could

0.10 take the path going left 30 m before the **Sávas Chapel** (right), traverse the stream and then go right on the country lane (see map).

In spring it is best to leave the road two minutes after the chapel at a concrete ford and go left, cross a second ford

0.15 and arrive at a walled **olive garden.**

> *Alternative:* If you want to take the easier route, go *left immediately* after the ford (out of the valley), pass a house (right) after 200 m and start climbing up to the right through a wooded area at the next fork. After two bends comes quite a long, straight upward stretch (AWT 0.25).

0.15 If you prefer to walk in the "old-fashioned way", you climb up to the right already at the olive garden, until you discover a path going right (**P1:** N37°47.716/E26°49.856′). This leads uphill to the right of a steep vineyard

0.20   ① and, **above** it without a path, over the ramps and steps of the retaining walls to the left-hand upper end of the olive grove lying above the vineyard. There you will find a

0.25   short, stony ascent to the **roadway** running immediately above it. If you follow this to the right, it becomes flatter, traverses an olive grove and passes below a right turn-off

0.35   ㉒. After 150 m a **stone path** (**P2:** N37°47.541'/E26°50.075', 210 m) leads you on up left. This is partly a newly laid, shady hiking trail – a small compensation for the destruction of the erstwhile mule track, which until 2004 ran from Vourliótes to the sea. The footpath leads up to the

0.45   new **country lane** (**P3:** N37°47.464'/ E26°50.247' 270 m),

0.50   which you take to the right until you reach a **fork.**

       Here you go up to the right – but only for 100 m! On the

!!   left an *old section of path* has survived the "land clearance" and brings you through thick bushes to a parting of the ways below an olive grove. Here you go left and at once reach a roadway, which you continue along straight

!!   ahead on the same level. After three minutes comes a left-

1.00   hand bend and, 10 m further on more *to the right,* a **defile** ② up to the cemetery (right). 150 m beyond that an alley

1.05   climbs up to the right, to the **Platía in Vourliótes,** a wonderful square with green and blue chairs, a meeting place for many hikers ③.

> *The overall appearance of **Vourliótes** is distinguished from that of other villages by the many "Turkish"-style oriels and porches made of timber. The builders came from Asia Minor, which at that time was still settled by the Greeks.*

To the right of the "blue chairs" is an alley which you ascend for two bends without steps, ignoring two car parks (left). On the asphalt road you first walk on the same level, then descending.

Whenever you see Kokkári and Vathí on the right, you have reached the right turn-off of the old paved path. From here the trail leads in the opposite direction to ㉒. Initially it runs along roadways, before continuing right on a proper paved

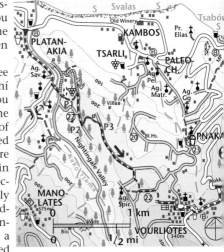

path. The shady pines ④ further out of the valley have

1.30 fallen victim to the 2000 forest fire. Cross a **roadway** diagonally to the right, and again later. Almost on the val-

1.50 ley bottom this **roadway** is crossed for a last time, in order to get down to the stream-bed. Having crossed the stream (possibly using a tree trunk), you go left and then head for the sea until you arrive at the first houses in

2.05 **Kokkári.**

㉒ The Power of Nature

This three to four-hour walk leads from Kokkári up to the pretty mountain village of Vourliótes and then back down to the sea via the nightingale valley. In the well frequented first section of the route you experience how nature has slowly reclaimed the region where a disastrous forest fire occurred.
It is not absolutely necessary to take along provisions since there are lovely inns in Vourliótes. From there one could as an alternative take the continuation described in ㉓.
■ *8.5 km, difference in altitude 340 m, moderate*

AWT
0.00 Strolling along the west beach in **Kokkári,** you reach the main street in twelve minutes. There, the **hotel "Milos Beach"** marks the beginning of this walk. At the wayside shrine near the hotel, walk uphill and then bear right at the fork before the high concrete wall, above the greenhouses with orchids on the right. The unusual arch you

0.07 later walk under is the aqueduct leading to an old **watermill** which used to be located under the vertical pipe on the right-hand side of the way.

30 m later you should give yourself a few minutes to enjoy the chapel of Áyios Ioánnis ① on the left above the way – and especially its magnificent location. Water is also available there.

0.10 Immediately you take a **path** on the right down to the stream bed, which in spring can be traversed via a tree trunk, otherwise on stones. The path leads to the left and then slightly uphill, but stays beneath the dirt road on the

right for a while. At a red diamond-shaped marking, it
0.15 leads up to the right and over the **dirt road** (**P1:**
N37°46.585'/ E26°52.473'). Diagonally across on the left
you continue walking uphill on steps. The path ②, which
is trodden into soft sandstone, leads through the area of
the disastrous forest fire of 2000 which destroyed the region on the south coast from here as far as Iréon ⑥. Following two very dry winters, the parched pines simply ig-
nited into flames like pieces of kindling wood. One third
of the wooded areas on Sámos was burned then. Meanwhile, the forest floor is green once again, and only the remains of the trees are still grey-black and bare ③. Especially white (= sage leaf) and violet (= grey-haired) rockroses
and mastic plants grow there exuberantly. Nature has
summoned all its forces to regenerate itself.

0.35 Later you come to a **dirt road** (**P2:** N37°47.025'/E26°
51.863') and cross it diagonally to the right. Three minutes later, now beneath pines, you cross it again and
change onto a footpath uphill. The footpath leads
through a stream bed where the trees were not as dried
out in 2000 and thus didn't burn. Afterwards, the wide
0.55 flagstone path crosses a **dirt road** and shortly after leads
to a newly paved section of the trail which you leave
again to the right 15 m later.

A paved street to the right comes next (**P3:** N37°47.172'/
1.00 E26°51.341'). After its junction with the **main street**,
walk to the left into the village, enjoying a great view of
Kokkári and the city of Sámos. Walk past a spring set in a
★ framework and a garden inn until you arrive at the main
1.10 square, the *platía* of **Vourliótes** with its lovely tavernas.
Getting to your feet again somewhat reluctantly after the

break, you leave the square beside the post office/bar (left) by entering a level alley ④ and, after the *"Blaue Quelle"*, come to a small well (right). Behind it you go down the alley in the direction of Manolátes and, at the electricity poles, left along the level alley.

	You pass the cemetery (left) and come to a wonderful de-
1.15	file ⑤. Further down you turn left into the **roadway** ini-
	tially running uphill (**P4:** N37°47.196′/E26°50.673′). In
!!	the ascending left-hand bend which follows after three
!!	minutes *you leave the roadway* by going right and, *after*
1.20	*10 m, right again at right angles* into a shady **forest path**
	(**P5:** N37°47,257′/E26°50,532′). Disregarding the turn-offs
	into the fields on either side, you reach a lane, drop down
1.25	to the right to a **fork** (**P6:** N37°47.339′/E26°50.431′) and
	there go left.
!!	After a short climb you continue more or less on the same
1.30	level as far as the *two steps* formed by the **bifurcation of a**
	path to the left ⑥ (**P7:** N37°47.468′/E26°50.244′). A new-
1.35	ly laid paved path soon runs past a **stone hut** (right) into
	an olive grove. Three minutes later it meets a roadway,
!!	which you take down to the right. *After 150 m* you follow
1.40	**vehicle tracks** leading left (**P8:** N37°47.561′/E26°50.044′)
	(Straight ahead would also take you to Platanákia.)
	In long loops, round a two-storey building, you arrive at
1.50	the bottom of the nightingale **valley** (**P9:** N37°47.565′/
	E26°49.822′). Here you take the broad forest path to the
1.55	right and march, later on the **road**, out of the valley past
2.05	the Sávas chapel to **Platanákia.** The bus stops at the gar-
	den inn on the main street. It comes past here about 20
	minutes after leaving Karlóvassi.

㉓ The thunderous one

Vrondá, at 450 years the oldest monastery on the island, is the highlight of the six to seven-hour hike along with the enchanting mountain village of Vourliótes. The ascent to 570 m is initially along roadways, later on paths. The stretch leading to the sea also includes old paved paths. A stop-off in Vourliótes is a must, in Pnaká maybe too.
■ *14 km, difference in altitude 460 m, difficult*

▷ Map see previous page

AWT   The old Vrondá monastery, which was partly burned down in 2005, lies hidden behind the Lazáros ridge above Kokkári ①.

0.00   With the portal of the large **church of Kokkári** behind you, set off on the concrete road, past a playground (left), as far as a T-junction. Here you go left and, shortly afterwards, right behind the pension "Angela". Having gone

0.05   left at the following fork, you cross the **bypass road.**
On the other side of the road you come to a wayside altar, take the path up right, then stroll straight ahead and later, below a chapel (left), right down through gardens. Thereafter you go uphill again and left into a steep, shady olive grove. After clambering over a few low walls there, you

0.15   end up above the grove on a **rural lane (P1: N37°46.450'/ E26°53.165').**
Follow it to the right, down into a dip, in which two walled vineyards are embedded. Between them you traverse the dip without a path. On the far side you ascend

0.20 on ruts to a transverse **lane** (**P2:** N 37°46.379'/E 26° 53.084'). Take it to the right, later climbing. In a right-hand bend you briefly glimpse the Ilías chapel. Further up

0.30 you come to a fairly major **roadway** (**P2:** N 37°46.286'/ E 26°53.058'), which you take to the right and, where it descends, passing by the Fotíni chapel (right) ②. 250 m

0.35 beyond that, near some houses, turn up left at the **cross-roads** (sign: Louloudes). The lusciously overgrown road-way heads towards the rugged rocks which you have to climb over.

!! At the fork after eight minutes do *not follow the signpost,*
!! but turn off *right* and then immediately climb *up left* to
!! the cruciform domed basilica of the Profítis Elías (in some maps also referred to as Ay. Georgios). Right beside it you find a path which runs up through the forest and past a pool (left). Above it you keep left and again come to the roadway (**P3:** N37°46.181'/E26°52.460', 150 m), which you follow further up.

Walking alongside a wire mesh fence, you pass the
0.50 **Dimítrios Chapel** standing above it to the left. The two following turn-offs downhill are of course of no interest to us summiteers. We continue on up round four tight bends and through olive groves, in which, at a distance of 100 m, stands a house on the left.

At last our intermediate goal comes into view: four dilapi-
1.00 dated **bathtubs**, a drinking trough (**P4:** N 37°46.239'/ E26° 52.270', 220 m). Here on the right begins the marked path ③ through the former forest. After ten minutes it fol-lows the wider, former forest path, which winds its way
1.15 up serpentine bends into a **saddle** (**P5:** N37°46.471'/E26° 52.037', 270 m).

Then the level path skirts the edge of the mountain. Be sure to look back! Later the path turns left, runs parallel

1.30 with a stream-bed (right), **crosses** it further up and climbs again on the other side, still above the stream. Initially

1.35 overgrown, the roadway heads **"inland"** to a fork (**P6:** N 37°46.554'/E 26°51.553'). The mighty cube of the monastery suddenly towers over the pilgrim.

(Died-in-the-wool pathfinders can push straight on here, rather laboriously following the markings through the ferns, but then eventually joining up again with the old, still passable path.)

The more careful hiker goes left on the roadway, then makes a short cut by going right 100 m before the road

1.55 and likewise arrives at **Vrondá Monastery.**

The fortress-like monastery from 1566 is consecrated to the "Holy Virgin of Thunder", as thunderstorms often occur in this region.

Four high residential wings surround the domed basilica standing in the middle, almost forming a square (p. 107). The basilica houses frescoes and a precious carved iconostasis. Hidden behind the residential arcades, moreover, is a Christ's Chapel. Following renovation the complex is only partially open to visitors; one monk now lives here again.

From the forecourt it is not far to the road, which you go down for six minutes. Shortly after a sharp right-hand bend a driveway drops to the left and, beyond the house, continues on down as a wide kalderími. Unfortunately you end up on the road again, which you also go down, past a chapel (left). 50 m after a left turn-off, though, you can leave it by taking a path to the left. Further down you descend the steps on the right and, in **Vourliótes**, along the first alley to the left, quickly reach the wonderful

2.15 **platía.**

Even if you have rested yourself on the "Blue Chairs", you then have to descend the steps next to the green chairs. The route takes you steeply downhill past the church (right). At the edge of the village, below the roadway, stands a house on the right. There you turn right at an acute angle down the old paved path, which is later traversed two more times by the new roadway. At the fork

2.30 beside the **bridge** you go right, down to **Pnaká** (p. 88 ④), where famous springs and yet another pretty inn await you. Right next to the inn the paved path continues downhill, forking after four minutes in front of a house.

Alternative: If you go left here, you come – past the chapel Ayía Matróna with important frescoes with scenes from Genesis from the 17th century – to **Kámbos** and the broad beach of Sválas (AWT 2.55)).

If you go *right,* you later cross the road and find, diagonally displaced by 15m to the left, a path and subsequently a beautiful paved path ④ leading down to the main road just outside **Avlákia.**

3.00

Proceed upward 100 m left to the bay of **Tsábou** with a restaurant. Running along the main road is the bus route, which has a stop here and in Avlákia, which also has a taverna.

Feast-Days – Panigíri

Often the hiker is fortunate enough to land completely unexpectedly in the middle of a religious festival. The church or chapel is bedecked with flags, a large congregation of guests in festive dress is sitting around – in their midst at least one priest. The tables are groaning under the weight of the food which the womanfolk or the owner of a private chapel have brought with them. Homemade drinks are offered; canned drinks are sold at cost price. Immediately the stranger is invited to taste the many dishes and is involved in a conversation. These are unforgettable Greek moments. The festivals take place on the name day of the patron saint of the church involved:

23rd April	Áyios Geórgios	20th July	Profítis Ilías
5th May	Ayía Iríni	26th July	Ayía Paraskeví
21st May	Áyios Konstantínos	27th July	Áyios Panteleímon
Ascension Day	Ayía Análipsi	6th August	Metamórphosis
Whitsuntide	Ayía Triáda	15thAugust	Assumption Day
24th June	Ay. Ioánnis Pródomos	29th August	Áyios Ioánnis
29th June	Ayii Apóstoli	1st Sept.	Áyios Mámas
7th July	Ayía Kyriakí	14th Sept.	Áyios Stavrós

㉔ Four chapels

... lie on the route of this three-hour circular tour through varied landscape. Walking along hidden paths and easily passable country lanes, the hiker gives Kokkári a wide berth. If one stays the course without taking a short cut, he or she finally reaches one of Kokkári's bays for bathing.

■ *7.5 km, diff. in altitude 120 m, easy to moderate*

AWT
0.00 The portal of the large **church in Kokkári** behind us, we set off on the concrete road, past a playground (left), as far as a T-junction. Here we go left, straight ahead at the turn-off beside the pension "Angela" and then in a right-hand
0.05 bend through to the **by-pass** (culvert).

On the other side we take the country lane and, after three minutes, turn right at the fork into a shady defile. At the next fork after 100 m we go left and proceed straight ahead. After a chicken coop (right) the roadway begins to
!! climb. After about 70 m – shortly *before a rock face* on the left – lies the entrance to a forest path on the left (**P1:** N37°46.281'/E26°53.213'). Having trekked through a fairly long, dense patch of forest, we come to a brighter olive
!! grove ①. Just beyond this on the right is the *turn-off* up to
0.20 the **Profítis Elías Chapel** ② between house ruins (**P2:** N37°46.196'/E26°53.173', 105 m). The magnificent view
★ of Kokkári makes it an ideal rest area.

Up above a wide track leads on uphill to a wide roadway, which we go down to the right. At the fork after 300 m we go left, first on the same level, later descending, past the
0.30 Fotíni Chapel (right, p. 97 ②), to the hamlet **Audites.**

At the fork there we turn left towards Loulóudas, heading for the blue chapel dome set in the dark green of the mountainside. Later the roadway climbs more steeply and comes to a large signposted fork. Here we go right and immediately find the second **Profítis Elías Chapel** (p. 105 ④) up on the left (**P3:** N37°46.246'/E26°52.555', 120 m). It is the oldest on today's tour and is – untypically, as in the case of the first one – not situated on a mountain top. (It is designated as a St. George's chapel in some maps.) Below it we continue straight along a country lane, almost without losing height, and go left at the fork above a house. At the next **fork** too we go left, but uphill into a forest in which stands a house on the left. Soon there is another **fork** (**P4:** N37°46.400'/E26°52.352', 120 m). Here we go down a lane to the right, but it ends after just three minutes; 30 m before that a trail on the right leads downhill ③, with house ruins on the right-hand side. The path swings to the left further down, running through the tree remains of the great fire in 2000. Using our modest pathfinding skills, we manage to negotiate rather thick vegetation until we come to a roadway, which we go down to the left to the **Panteleímonas Chapel** (**P5:** N37°46.596'/E26°52.337', 45 m). It lies somewhat concealed – even before the stream-bed – on the left in the forest and has a beautiful pebble floor. The Mána spring further upstream is not very interesting.

We traverse the concrete ford and immediately go up right on a roadway. About 50 m after the end of the guardrails a path on the right leads down to Kokkári, a possible short cut (see page 92).

The roadway leads up over a hilltop. Upon descending

0.40

0.45

0.50

1.00

again, now on asphalt, we stay above a fairly large cluster
1.15 of holiday houses and later go left below the **Kalidon Hotel.** Where the hotel building finishes, we turn left and do so again in front of the large holiday house which follows. Now the asphalt roadway climbs slightly, passes a solar
1.25 plant (right) and soon arrives at the **Fanoúris Chapel** ④. From its terrace we enjoy the fantastic view of Kokkári.

From here we continue on grass as far as the remains of a roadway, which we take down to the right. Later we proceed without a path down through the grass of an olive
1.30 grove to the **main road.**

So as not to have to drop steeply down to Tsamadoú Bay (and especially not back up again), we walk down the road 400 metres to the right and have our bathing break
1.35 at **Lemonákia Bay.** There two inns await our arrival and, afterwards, another 15 minutes along the pavement to
1.50 the edge of **Kokkári.**

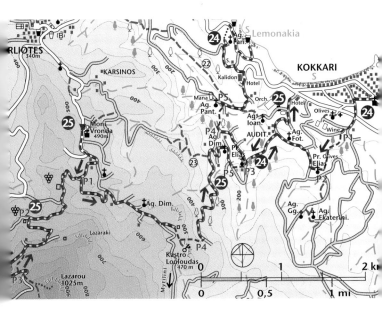

㉕ Oh Lazarus!

Today we do what all the beach tourists in Kokkári dream of doing: climbing the "local mountain" Lazárou! That will take us nine to ten hours, though, mostly on the vintners' roadways and two stretches of path. As there are no proper springs, it is wise to take water – and a windcheater too.
It is possible to shorten the tour considerably and just visit the Kástro Louloúdas.
■ *18 km, difference in altitude 1025 m, difficult*

▷ *Map see previous page*

AWT   Today we splash out on the roughly 16 Euro taxi ride from Kokkári to **Moní Vrondá** (490 m) (p. 107). In the monastery church, to the left of the entrance, it is possible to see the Martyrdom of Saint Lazarus; we shall just have to see what sufferings lie in store for us on Lazarus' mountain.

0.00   From **monastery portal** you go up some steps to the street and there left, heading towards the two Lazarus' peaks ①. After six minutes you leave the asphalt in a right-hand bend and come to a country lane on the left. At the next fork below three houses you march up to the right and on past the uppermost houses until you come to

0.15   a wide **roadway** (**P1**: N37°46.093'/E26°51.203', 575 m). Make a good mental note of this point for the way back! Here go up to the right, past a concrete structure (a loading ramp?) to a fork and there left.

On a flatter stretch you finally have a chance to appreci-

ate the wonderful landscape with the steeply terraced vineyards. Down on the coast lies Platanákia, embedded in the side of the mountain on the left is Stavrinídes and below it, half hidden, pretty Manolátes. You soon reach a large fork (**P2:** N37°45.810'/E26°50.781') and an altitude of 720 metres. Following the sign to the left, still in the midst of terraced vineyards, you proceed as far as an orchard, on the right-hand side of which stands an imposing house 2. Beside the driveway to this house is a water tank and, 50 m beyond that, you see where a path turns off to the left – you will later be using it from above. Climbing, you continue straight ahead and also where the road then makes a **right turn-off**, always in the direction of Pyrgos. At the next fork you go left – for who on earth wants to go to Kioulafides?

0.55

After this bend you see the next challenge: Lazarus' back. The start of the climb is soon reached. Immediately where the sharp right-hand bend ends below a strip of scree at the foot of the Big Lazárou, you find where the climb starts (**P3:** N37°45.449'/E26°50.831', 925 m).

In the absence of a proper trail a number of routes to the **summit of Lazárou** are marked by cairns. The position at 1,025 m above sea level affords a commanding view of the island. This location also lent itself to the construction of a fortified refuge, but nothing remains to be seen of it. Lazárou is the third highest peak on Sámos. The second highest is just behind you, Profítis Elías with the radar reflectors for the ships at sea.

1.35

The descent is again through gravelly rock as far as the **roadway** and the first bend. The easier, but longer way is the one you already know. Because it is simpler to identify

1.55

paths from above, we want to risk the short cut, although it is not maintained properly since the 2000 fire. In the upper part you keep slightly left; in the thicket you follow the path which a worried trekking book author cut away in 2012 and thus arrive back at the **roadway** next to the water tank, where you go right. The paths to the Small Lazarus (Lazaráki) are no longer traceable – so stay on the same track. After the two left turn-offs and the "loading ramp" you reach the **point "P1"** again.

2.05

2.40

Short cut: The descent from the Kástro Loulóudas is rather gravelly and calls for surefootedness. One could now set off on the way home to Moní Vrondá.

Otherwise one perseveres straight on down and, after a wide left-hand bend, takes the signposted **right turn-off** to Mytiliní. At a fork you walk right on a concrete track, past the Dimitrios Chapel ③ and into the saddle between the Lazaráki (right) and a rock formation. Here you use the **left turn-off** and then proceed in the same direction between a shed (left) and a drinking trough until beneath the Kástro rock.

2.45

3.00

*The few remains of the walls of the **Kástro Loulóudas** can be reached in about eight minutes – but only if you are free from giddiness! This strategically important rock was already inhabited in ancient times. In the 13th century AD it was fortified again and afforded the population protection against raids.*

Directly in front of the rock, look for the markings which show the stony path to the left across the slope covered with scree. It runs down into a green plateau, **swings** left shortly before doing so (**P4:** N37°45.656'/E26°52.192', 470 m) and peters out into vehicle tracks. These lead you to the forest road, which you now follow in the direction of the sea. Initially still through burned terrain, then through a pine forest and past the famous **four bathtubs**, the hiker's landmark ㉓. Just beyond the Dimitri Chapel you can start looking for the short cut (**P5:** N 37°46,181'/E 26°52,460') to **Profítis Elías Chapel** ④ on the left. (It is also designated as a St. George's chapel in some maps.)

3.15

3.40

4.00

4.20

More or less exhausted you end up in **Kokkári** and proudly peer up at the summit. Just like the beach tourists do too.

Moní Vrondá

Overview   Übersicht

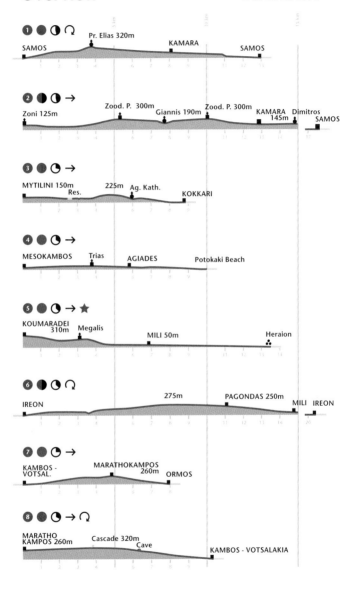

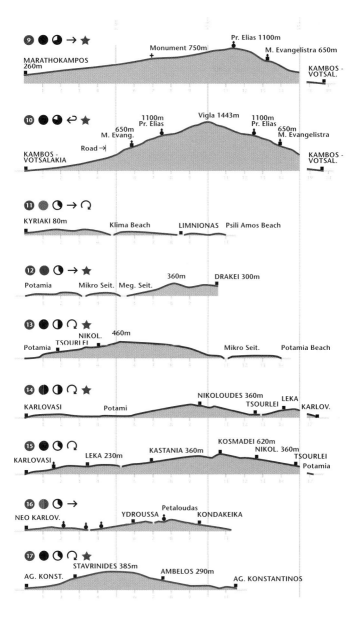

9 ● ◐ → ★

MARATHOKAMPOS 260m — Monument 750m — Pr. Elias 1100m — M. Evangelistra 650m — KAMBOS - VOTSAL.

10 ● ◐ ⇐ ★

KAMBOS - VOTSALAKIA — Road → — M. Evang. 650m — Pr. Elias 1100m — Vigla 1443m — Pr. Elias 1100m — M. Evangelistra 650m — KAMBOS - VOTSAL.

11 ● ◐ → ↻

KYRIAKI 80m — Klima Beach — LIMNIONAS — Psili Amos Beach

12 ● ◐ → ★

Potamia — Mikro Seit. — Meg. Seit. — 360m — DRAKEI 300m

13 ● ◑ ↻ ★

Potamia — TSOURLEI — NIKOL. — 460m — Mikro Seit. — Potamia Beach

14 ◐ ◑ ↻ ★

KARLOVASI — Potami — NIKOLOUDES 360m — TSOURLEI — LEKA — KARLOV.

15 ● ◐ ↻

KARLOVASI — LEKA 230m — KASTANIA 360m — KOSMADEI 620m — NIKOL. 360m — TSOURLEI — Potamia

16 ◐ ◐ →

NEO KARLOV. — YDROUSSA — Petaloudas — KONDAKEIKA

17 ● ◐ ↻ ★

AG. KONST. — STAVRINIDES 385m — AMBELOS 290m — AG. KONSTANTINOS

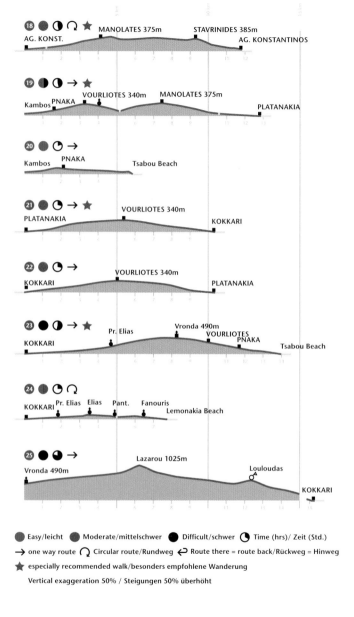

18 ⬤ ◐ ↻ ★ MANOLATES 375m   STAVRINIDES 385m
AG. KONST.   AG. KONSTANTINOS

19 ◐ ◐ → ★   VOURLIOTES 340m   MANOLATES 375m
Kambos PNAKA   PLATANAKIA

20 ⬤ ◔ →
Kambos PNAKA   Tsabou Beach

21 ⬤ ◔ → ★   VOURLIOTES 340m
PLATANAKIA   KOKKARI

22 ⬤ ◔ →   VOURLIOTES 340m
KOKKARI   PLATANAKIA

23 ⬤ ◑ → ★   Pr. Elias   Vronda 490m   VOURLIOTES
KOKKARI   PNAKA   Tsabou Beach

24 ⬤ ◑ ◔ ↻   Pr. Elias Elias Pant. Fanouris
KOKKARI   Lemonakia Beach

25 ⬤ ◕ →   Lazarou 1025m   Louloudas
Vronda 490m   KOKKARI

⬤ Easy/leicht ⬤ Moderate/mittelschwer ⬤ Difficult/schwer ◔ Time (hrs)/ Zeit (Std.)

→ one way route ↻ Circular route/Rundweg ⇌ Route there = route back/Rückweg = Hinweg

★ especially recommended walk/besonders empfohlene Wanderung

Vertical exaggeration 50% / Steigungen 50% überhöht

Some Greek words for hikers:

Stress on the accents.

jássas	**hello**	kerós	**weather**
ne	yes	aéras	wind
óchi	no	meltémi	strong north wind
parakaló	please	ílios	sun
efcharistó	thank you	wrochí	rain
endáxi	okay	omíchli	fog
sto kaló	all the best		
kalá	lovely	níssos	**island**
símera	today	farángi, langádi	ravine, gorge
ávrio	tomorrow	kámpos, pláka	plains
pósin óra?	How long?	livádi	meadow
pósso makriá	How far is it to...?	déndro	tree
ine ja?		léfkes	poplars
puíne...?	Where is...?	dássos	forest
óra	hour	lófos	hill
neró	water	wounó, óros	mountain
psomí	bread	vígla	mountain peak
tirí	cheese	vráches	rock, cliff
míkro	small	spíleo	cave
mégalo	big	thálassa	sea
leoforió	bus	órmos	bay
stásis	bus stop	límni	lake
enikáso	rent	potámi	river
aftókinito	auto	réma	dry bed
mechanáki	motor bike	pigí	spring
podílato	bicycle	pérazma	pass, ridge
kaíki	boat	xirolithía	dry wall
hora	**city**	odiporió	**wandering**
horio	hamlet	isía	straight on
spíti	house	dexiá	right
platía	square	aristerá	left
parélia	harbour promenade	apáno	uphill
kástro	Venetian castle	káto	downhill
pírgos	fortified Venetian castle	kondá	near
		makriá	far
nekrotafío	cemetery	ásfalto	asphalt street
limáni	harbour	drómos	street
vrísi	fountain	chomaódromos	gravel street
stérna	cistern	dasikí odós	forest path
kafenío	café, village assembly	odós	path
		skála	path of steps
eklisiá	**church**	monopáti	mule track
papás	priest	kalderími	paved way
moní, monastíri	monastery	katsikó drómos	goat path
ksoklísi	chapel	yéfira	bridge
panagía	Mother of God	stavrodrómi	crossing, intersection
panigíri	parish fair		
ágios, agía, AG	saint	hártis	map
ikonostasio	icon altar screen	kutrúmbulo	path marking
katholikón	central building in a monastery	phrygana	scrub, the island hiker's enemy

Abbreviations, Key

▬▬▬▬	hiking route on a road or dirt track
▬▬▬▬	hiking route on a street
― ― ― ― ― ▪	hiking route on a path
·············	hiking route without a path
▁ᴬᴸᵀ▁ₒₒₒₒₒ	alternative route, short-cut
← ⇐	walking direction / alternative
	GPS point
══════	street
▬▬▬▬	dirt track, sandy track
▬MP ▯▬	monopáti, mule track / marking
— — –	dry stream-bed (at times), hollow
🌿	antenna
Ⓑ ⁝B⁝	bus stop / seasonal
Ⓟ	parking area
Ⓗ	helicopter landing pad
⊞	cemetery
+	wayside shrine, monument
⬭	sports field
∩	cave
♜ ♟	medieval castle, dwelling tower / ruins
🏛	ancient ruins, statue
▪ ▫	houses / ruins
♟ ♟	monastery, large church / ruins
♟ ♟ ♟	chapel / summit chapel / ruins
▽ ▽	taverna / open seasonally
✳ ☼	windmill/watermill, ruins
�ြ ▫ ▫	fountain, well, spring, reservoir, cistern
S	swimming possible

In the text:

!!	pay attention to turn-off!
↙	possible feelings of vertigo
OW	time for walking one way
★	the author's 18 favourite spots